The SOUTH PACIFIC Companion

J. C. WILLIAMSON THEATRES offer an ENCHANTED EVENING in the . . . "South Pacific"

The SOUTH PACIFIC Companion

LAURENCE MASLON

A Fireside Book

Published by Simon & Schuster
New York • London • Toronto • Sydney

Fireside
A Division of Simon & Schuster, Inc.
1230 Avenue of the Americas
New York, NY 10020

First Fireside hardcover edition June 2008

FIRESIDE and colophon are registered trademarks of Simon & Schuster, Inc.

For information about special discounts for bulk purchases, please contact Simon & Schuster
Special Sales at 1-800-456-6798 or business@simonandschuster.com

Designed by Louise Leffler at Sticks Design

Printed and bound by SNP Leefung, China

10 9 8 7 6 5 4 3 2 1

Library of Congress Cataloging-in-Publication Data

ISBN-13: 978-1-4165-7313-5
ISBN-10:   1-4165-7313-5

To Fritz Brun,

for his friendship, wisdom, and Continental charm

PAGE 1: A handbill for the Australian production of South Pacific.

PAGES 2–3: The coast of the island of Espiritu Santo, the site of South Pacific.

PAGE 5: Mary Martin and Ezio Pinza: the reprise of "Some Enchanted Evening."

ABOVE: One of Broadway's greatest hits, packing them in at the Majestic.

Contents

FOREWORD BY
ADAM GUETTEL

Right now. In your mind. Listen to the first three notes of "Bali Ha'i." And again. Now faster. You are hearing the overture of *South Pacific*. As these three notes accelerate and bear down on us we feel we are being led into a landscape of enormous breadth. The gesture is so wide! Perhaps that first octave leap is all it takes to bring that feeling forth. But I doubt the leap would feel like a leap at all if not for the note which follows. That third note. That insinuating half-step is so very efficient. It sets a spring. Musical tension is like a battery in story telling. It stores energy for release. But how is this energy channeled? Through whom? Through what theme?

I don't think Rodgers and Hammerstein ever said, "Quick! Let's do *South Pacific*. We can make a statement about miscegenation!" Or, "How about *Carousel*? The lyric complexity of spousal abuse!" They were story guys and story and character came first. They knew they couldn't write, day after day, a noble philosophy. There's no stuffing in it. And noble is slippery. Noble one day is self serving the next. And how could they choose to hang an entertainment on socio/politics when in 1949—and certainly in 2007—we are smashed over the head with it all day. No. Audiences are engaged and musicals are sung by people with lives and prejudice. And yes, we have to be carefully taught.

In our time, a nagging question about *South Pacific* tends to be, "How could a whole story, how could a whole musical hinge on a woman's decision to embrace a man with bi-racial children?" Holding racist beliefs isn't just holding the thought, it's having internalized the stakes behind the thought and what are those stakes? Why are we, what are we afraid of? Down inside of us, what is racism? Is it like being in an early childhood state? A sort of "all mine" world view in which the fruits of this earth will not be shared by anyone who is not…me! And then, as the confidence of holding a majority stake is inexorably worn down by the wind and water of real life, do we try to protect what we think we are losing? Is Nellie like that? Or is she even more naïve?

This is the lyric that Hammerstein originally wrote for Nellie and Emile in the spot where "A Cockeyed Optimist" now comes:

NELLIE
The sky is a bright canary yellow,
And the sea is a robin's-egg blue.
It makes you wish,
When you fall asleep,
You will dream about the view.

EMILE
Bizarre and improbable and pretty
As a page from the fairy-tale books,
It makes you wish
That the world could be
As lovely as it looks.

Director Josh Logan said that it was cut (and replaced by "Optimist") because Rodgers and Hammerstein realized Nellie wouldn't know the world wasn't as lovely as it appeared to her. Her discovery of this fact (and the confrontation of the racism within her) is Nellie's story in the play.

Are we just as naïve in America, even today, as we stand at the global altar, concurrently rejecting and embracing new faces? In our national mind and on our conscience we can hear the first three notes of *South Pacific* heralding again and again the foreignness and the familiarity of what we face, the potential and the risk. If music can store energy, it can release it.

Adam Guettel's works for the musical theater include *Floyd Collins* and *The Light in the Piazza*.

INTRODUCTION

Musicals get written for a variety of reasons. Sometimes a story strikes the collective fancy of the creators. Sometimes an actor identifies a role that would be perfect to be musicalized. Sometimes an idea comes to a producer who gathers an artistic group together and creates a show. Sometimes a member of a creative team puts a notion forward and hopes to inspire his teammates. Sometimes there is something compelling about a time and a place that makes a certain story need to be told.

It is this last thought that best describes *South Pacific*. No other musical in history has ever been so "at the right place at the right time." As we look back from nearly sixty years out, astonishment comes from seeing just how many pieces of the artistic puzzle fit together so beautifully. Perhaps the audiences who saw the production in its original incarnation assumed it was all effortless. It was anything but, and the real story is just how hard all the creators worked—and successfully—to create a musical play that stood alone in the middle of the twentieth century both as an embodiment of the American spirit, and as an indication of how far the American musical had come as a bona fide art form. This book tells that story.

Larry Maslon has chosen to explain the creation of *South Pacific* in a unique way. The musical premiered in 1949, and he takes the four major collaborators—James Michener, Richard Rodgers, Oscar Hammerstein II, and Joshua Logan—from December 7, 1941—"a day that will live in infamy"—following them through the ensuing

decade. At the same time, he gives us a glimpse of what was happening in the world throughout that tumultuous period. His reasoning is simple: *South Pacific* tells a story based in World War II, and everyone connected with the show was affected by that war. For Rodgers and Hammerstein, their first collaboration, *Oklahoma!*, had captured the essence of the America that the country was fighting for. With Michener, his original material was based on experiences he had while stationed in the South Pacific. As for Joshua Logan, his military service informed his theatrical viewpoint. As Maslon describes, the timeliness of all this had resonance as to how this particular musical got written, when it got written, and why it was received with such acclaim.

For the still relatively new team of Richard Rodgers and Oscar Hammerstein II, *South Pacific* was a threshold. It was their fourth Broadway show, and although their first two—*Oklahoma!* and *Carousel*—had been embraced both by audiences and critics, their third was not. Titled *Allegro*, it was an entirely original story, told in bold and innovative theatrical ways. While it had a respectable initial run, *Allegro* divided the critics and the audiences, and the naysayers reacted with passion. Clearly Rodgers and Hammerstein felt stung by the reaction. For the team of Rodgers and Hammerstein to continue to be a major force, whatever show followed *Allegro* would have to be a hit.

And their way of making a hit was perhaps the opposite of what one might think: they pushed themselves ever further. They chose a contemporary story, ripped from the headlines. They wrote it for two stars. They used no choreography. And in Joshua Logan they took on a theater artist of equal stature. Nothing was taken for granted. And as a result, everyone did extraordinary work.

In my years as the President of The Rodgers and Hammerstein Organization, I have seen many *South Pacific*s. I have seen traditional productions in tours and light opera companies. I have seen it in Danish. I have seen it done by fine theaters that had never done a musical. I have even seen it withstand a production set in a rehabilitation ward (part of therapy for returning soldiers, you see…) And I have also seen the one existing piece of

OPPOSITE: Ted Chapin, in 1984, with Mrs Richard Rodgers, Mary Martin, and Mrs Oscar Hammerstein at the opening of a Richard Rodgers exhibit in New York.

ABOVE: The first scene of South Pacific from the original production in full color; notice the oversized frangipani surrounding the gazebo, left, as described in the opening scene directions.

film of Mary Martin and Ezio Pinza together. It shows what an amazing—and sexy—pair those two made!

As I write this, there is a new and exciting production planned for Lincoln Center Theater in New York that is touched upon in the last chapter of this book. The care and intelligence taken by a crew of today's premiere theater artists, and the discoveries they are all making as they dive into this show, is another indication of the staying power of *South Pacific*.

One final note: since *South Pacific* proved to be a monumental experience for everyone involved, the stories surrounding the original production have been told time and again, in books and in interviews. The original collaborators were all good storytellers, but the versions don't quite agree. Larry Maslon has made a rule for himself to find the earliest known telling of a given story, with the theory that it will probably be the most accurate. That, in addition to first class research, lets him tell this story more completely than it has ever been told.

Ted Chapin, New York City
November 2007

CLOCKWISE FROM BOTTOM LEFT: A bevy of Nellies: the very first, Mary Martin, in a signed portrait to Dick Rodgers; a costume sketch by Catherine Zuber for the 2008 Broadway revival; and the cinematic Mitzi Gaynor, 1958.

I wish I could tell you about the South Pacific.
The way it actually was. The endless ocean.
The infinite specks of coral we called islands.
Coconut palms nodding gracefully toward the ocean.
Reefs upon which waves broke into spray, and inner
lagoons, lovely beyond description.
I wish I could tell you about the sweating jungle,
the full moon rising behind the volcanoes,
and the waiting. The waiting. The timeless,
repetitive waiting.

But whenever I start to talk about the South Pacific,
people intervene.

James A. Michener, *Tales of the South Pacific*

PART ONE: THE PACIFIC THEATER

CHAPTER ONE
1941

On the morning of December 7, 1941, the voluminous Sunday *New York Times* thudded onto doormats all over the island of Manhattan.

It was, on the East Coast, a slow news day. If you were interested in show business, as a good many New Yorkers were, you might turn to the Arts section, where the theater column, "Gossip of the Rialto," sported an exciting headline: Irving Berlin, the master composer-lyricist of Broadway, was planning a return to his Music Box Theatre in the summer with an ambitious three-act revue, mixing some of his classic tunes with fresh new songs and sketches. This was big news—it had been nearly a decade since Berlin had brought a new revue to Broadway. Things were looking good for 1942.

When James A. Michener picked up his *New York Times* off the doormat of his small West Village apartment that morning, it is quite possible that he, too, turned first to the Arts section. While studying for his Master's degree at the Colorado State College of Education during the 1930s, Michener had become an ardent theater fan. Whenever he could, he went to Denver to see the productions being put on by the WPA's Federal Theatre Project. "Nothing was more important to my life than this theater," he would claim years later. Michener was also an opera fan, who listened avidly to the Saturday radio broadcasts from the Metropolitan Opera. There was one singer in particular who thrilled him, an Italian basso named Ezio Pinza. In the apartment that he shared with his wife, Michener had several stacks of bargain-basement 78s featuring Pinza.

It is also quite possible that Michener turned first to the *Times Book Review*. Only a year earlier, he had quit his job as an associate professor at Colorado State College to become a social sciences textbook editor for the prestigious Macmillian Publishing Company, located on Fifth Avenue. Michener's job was by no means glamorous—he packaged textbooks and assessed their financial viability—but at least the job was in publishing, and it was in New York. It was exciting to be even on the fringes of the literary scene, for Michener had written only a few articles about education for various scholarly journals. He had recently branched out, writing a surprisingly passionate piece in favor of America entering the war in Europe. So, perhaps he glanced at the first page of the newspaper to see what news there was of the conflict overseas.

However, if anyone in Manhattan was going to turn to the theater page first, it was Richard Rodgers. From his Upper East Side apartment, Rodgers would have read of Berlin's news with a combination of admiration and envy. With the possible exception of Cole Porter, in the early 1940s, Berlin was Rodgers' only real competition as the most successful composer on Broadway. And, as far as Rodgers was concerned, Berlin and Porter were luckier— they also wrote their own lyrics, while Rodgers had to wait for his talented but indolent partner, Lorenz Hart, to show up for work. The diminutive Hart was Broadway's darling, renowned for his trenchant, puckish wit, but the ambitious Rodgers was always eager to begin the next project and Larry Hart's lack of punctuality and dedication threatened to derail their partnership.

By any objective standpoint, Rodgers had little to complain about as 1941 drew to a close. Only a year before, he and Hart had concocted *Pal Joey*, the most sophisticated and adult musical ever to hit the Great White Way, but for Rodgers, who had averaged two shows a year for the last few seasons, it was not only frustrating to be without a show on the boards for 1941, it was embarrassing. Luckily, plans were underway for a new show for spring 1942, a musical adaptation of *The Warrior's Husband*, a saucy spoof of sexual politics in Ancient Greece. The classical setting provided just the kind of intelligent humor associated with Rodgers and Hart, and its racy premise did not hurt, either. Broadway's premiere comic dancer Ray Bolger was to star, in his first stage role in New York since he tickled movie audiences in *The Wizard of Oz*. Casting sessions for the rest of

PAGE 14: The date after the date that will live in infamy. At a Manhattan newsstand, the Daily Mirror announces the news that will change the world, December 8, 1941.

ABOVE: James A. Michener, textbook editor for Macmillan and occasional essayist.

the company were to begin later in December, and if Rodgers was apprehensive about Hart, he was enthusiastic about his other two collaborators, both of whom had served him and his work well in several previous projects—the producer Dwight Deere Wiman and the director Joshua Logan.

Josh Logan was one of Broadway's more successful younger directors, equally adept at plays and musicals. Broadway musicals of the late 1930s did not require a visionary director, but rather a craftsman who could get the piece up, deal with the stars' egos, and mine the script and score for laughs. Logan, a towering, Princeton-educated Southerner, was more than equal to these tasks. He had mounted two earlier shows with Rodgers and Hart, a fantastical romance called *I Married an Angel*, and an "Upstairs/Downstairs" satire, *Higher and Higher*, for which he had also cowritten the book. No one would claim that either show was a top-drawer musical comedy—not even Logan—but getting Rodgers' professional approval was no easy task, so the composer's offer to direct the Ray Bolger musical was extremely welcome.

ABOVE: As the 1940s began, there was no more successful songwriting team on Broadway than lyricist Lorenz Hart and composer Richard Rodgers.

ABOVE: Joshua Logan, center, surrounded by his colleagues from the University Players, 1932. Counterclockwise from upper left: Myron McCormick, Henry Fonda, Margaret Sullavan, and Barbara O'Neill. Fonda and Sullavan would be briefly married, as would Logan and O'Neill; both McCormick and Fonda would figure prominently in Logan's theatrical fortunes in the late 1940s.

OPPOSITE: In the 1920s, he was the wonder boy of Broadway; in the 1940s, he would achieve unprecedented career eminence. In between, however, Oscar Hammerstein II would face some very lean years.

PAGES 20–21: Late night bulletin, December 7, 1941. Crowds in Times Square watch the "Zipper"—the automated news headlines—for the shocking news from Pearl Harbor. The soldiers would be immediately summoned back for active duty.

Logan needed the work—he had been professionally out of commission for most of 1941, having spent the year in and out of mental hospitals and treatment facilities. Logan suffered from what we now call manic depression and his elliptical mood swings from elation to despair had worried his mother, his wife, and his colleagues. Soon after directing a successful revival of the British farce *Charley's Aunt* in the fall of 1940, he suffered a nervous breakdown. Over his strong objections, his family brought in a psychiatrist to guide his recovery. At that time, mental illness was rarely acknowledged—much less discussed—in public. To broadcast his condition would have been career suicide for Logan and although most of the theatrical community knew of his trials, the newspapers had not caught on to it yet. Despite Logan's breakdown, Rodgers wanted him again—and that was an immense boost to his confidence. He could not wait to get cracking.

Given his mood on the morning of December 7, Oscar Hammerstein II could be forgiven for not opening his copy of the *New York Times* at all. Only two days earlier, the newspaper had dismissed his latest Broadway show, a return to the operetta form called *Sunny River*, set in nineteenth-century New Orleans. Hammerstein had written the book and lyrics to Sigmund Romberg's music in addition to staging the mammoth show. The *Times* drama critic, Brooks Atkinson, had called *Sunny River* "workmanlike," the music "ponderous and pedestrian," and the entire enterprise "a duty call on entertainment." That was one of the better reviews. During the show's late November tryout in New Haven, Connecticut, the producer, Max Gordon, called in his old friend, the renowned comic dramatist and play doctor George S. Kaufman to see if anything could be done to improve it. Kaufman brought along his teenage daughter, Anne, and as the dreary train wheezed along the tracks northward in the November chill, she turned to her father and said, "Oh, daddy, this is awful. It's cold and it's miserable and it's Thanksgiving and we're not even going to have any turkey." "Just wait," replied Kaufman.

Kaufman's words were prophetic; *Sunny River* would limp through the rest of December, then vanish. Hammerstein was simply stumped. In the 1920s, he had been the golden boy of Broadway, with one commercial success after another, culminating in the groundbreaking *Show Boat* with Jerome Kern in 1927. His shows of the 1930s, however, were not built to last, even though they

yielded beautiful songs such as "All the Things You Are" and "The Song is You." He spent much of the decade, grudgingly, in Hollywood, but his career there had been tedious and uninspiring. Two decades earlier, Hammerstein had invigorated the operetta form; now it was burying him. "I have no plans and at the moment I don't feel like making any," he wrote to a friend after the *Sunny River* opening. Hammerstein began to think that he should retire for a while to his beautiful farm, down among the rolling hills and languorous cows in Bucks County, Pennsylvania. At least there he would not be reminded of his bomb down at the St. James Theatre.

By the morning of December 8, bombs of a theatrical nature were of no concern to the American public. The news from Pearl Harbor had blazed across the time zones to the East Coast and proclaimed a horrifying reality. Nearly four hundred Japanese warplanes had executed a sneak attack on the United States Pacific Fleet the previous

morning. Within two hours, eight American battleships were lost or damaged; three destroyers lost or damaged; the Army's Air Corps flying divisions were almost completely wiped out; and more than 2,400 servicemen and civilians were killed. Overnight, the Japanese High Command had declared war on the United States and Great Britain; and, later on the afternoon of December 8, President Franklin D. Roosevelt asked Congress to declare war on the Empire of Japan; they obliged. The world was now at war.

James Michener, Richard Rodgers, Josh Logan, and Oscar Hammerstein II were each leading separate lives on the island of Manhattan. But after December 7, they had to put their passions and preoccupations aside, as would millions of other Americans. The news of that day would eventually bring them all together, their fates intertwined around an island as far away from Manhattan as it could possibly be and still be on the planet earth—an island in the South Pacific.

A COCKEYED OPTIMIST

When the sky is a bright canary yellow
I forget ev'ry cloud I've ever seen—
So they call me a cockeyed optimist,
Immature and incurably green!

I have heard people rant and rave and bellow
That we're done and we might as well be dead—
But I'm only a cockeyed optimist,
And I can't get it into my head.

    I hear the human race
    Is falling on its face
    And hasn't very far to go,
    But ev'ry whippoorwill
    Is selling me a bill
    And telling me it just ain't so!

I could say life is just a bowl of jello
And appear more intelligent and smart,
But I'm stuck, like a dope,
With a thing called hope,
And I can't get it out of my heart!
                Not this heart!

Oscar Hammerstein was always keen to point out that the first ten minutes of any musical determines its fate. In *South Pacific*, he tells the audience almost immediately that, for all the exoticism of the setting, the real key to the musical is personal. "Think globally, act locally" would become a common populist saying in American politics, but the first song in the stage version of *South Pacific* puts it into dramatic practice.

Once Hammerstein decided to open the musical *sotto voce*, as it were (the film version and the 2001 television version make full use of their respective mediums by staging the opening on a much broader canvas), he and Rodgers had to take us inside the personalities of their leading characters, Nellie Forbush and Emile de Becque. The first attempt at musicalizing their thoughts came in the form of a philosophical travelogue called "Bright Canary Yellow":

NELLIE
The sky is a bright canary yellow,
And the sea is a robin's-egg blue.
It makes you wish,
When you fall asleep,
You will dream about the view.

EMILE
Bizarre and improbable and pretty
As a page from the fairy-tale books,
It makes you wish
That the world could be
As lovely as it looks.

Beautiful, poetic, even verging on the existential, but not particularly personal. The final version puts these sentiments back into Nellie's character, where they belong. (It was billed as "Not This Heart" during the show's tryout period.) Her essential optimism is juxtaposed against a world view—perhaps more prevalent in 1948 when the song was written than in 1943 when the show is set—that is cynical and pessimistic. As Nellie says in the dialogue before the song:

You know, I don't think we're at the end of the world like everybody else thinks. I can't work myself up to getting that low. . . . You know what they call me? Knucklehead Nellie. I guess I am, but I just can't help it.

During the second year of her run in *South Pacific*, Mary Martin was asked by the *New York Times* to recount her experiences in the show. A good deal had changed after the ebullience of her first year, she wrote; the recent war in Korea had given the show "a sharp new meaning. Under the impact of events, it turned a series of war recollections, softened by time and gilded by glamour, into a picture of grim contemporary reality." Martin thought of the young men dying in Korea ("the real thing—the best we have"), the "little Joe Cables," and of her own son, Larry Hagman, who was of draft age. "Sometimes," she continued, "when the news was bad I'd find it rather difficult to sing 'A Cockeyed Optimist.' But the qualities of strength inherent in *South Pacific* always lifted me again by the end of the performance."

There are few lyrics by Hammerstein that sum up his personal philosophy quite so well. In the early 1950s, Ed Sullivan referred to Hammerstein as a "cockeyed optimist" in his theater column for the *Daily News* and set Hammerstein's views against the prevailing negativism of the current Broadway scene. He contrasted Hammerstein's eternal sunniness with some of the darker aspects of Tennessee Williams' plays and extracted a quote from Hammerstein: "There is no more validity to the belief that life is one great snake pit than to the idea it was all one huge sunlit meadow."

In the score to *South Pacific*, there are only twenty-nine bars in which Nellie and Emile sing together; the reprise of the lines "I could say life is just a bowl of jello" through "not this heart." The stage direction says that they sing it in playful harmony ("*Sweet Adeline* fashion") and it shows how the two of them have completely embraced Nellie's (and Hammerstein's) philosophy. Ironically, it is the moment right before Nellie learns the truth about Emile's two children. The two of them are so harmonious at this point that even Emile de Becque, who has lived on a remote South Pacific island for a quarter of a century, can sing happily about "Jell-o"—a commercial product introduced only to the American market.

CHAPTER TWO
1942

I n military parlance, "theater of war" refers to the broad base of action where two opposing forces are joined in battle. As far as the American forces were concerned at the beginning of 1942, the Pacific Theater required a lot of improvisation.

Within two months of the attack on Pearl Harbor, the Empire of Japan had quickly, efficiently, and mercilessly extended its power in the Pacific over an area vaster than any other in human history. Japan had naval supremacy as far north as the Aleutian Islands; as far east (nearly) as Hawaii; as far south as New Guinea, only a few hundred miles from the coast of Australia; and had land forces as far west on mainland Asia as Inner Mongolia and Siam. They had driven American and British forces out of such strongholds as the Philippines, Malaya, and the Solomon Islands, and their navy was threatening Australia and New Zealand. Japan's sphere of influence covered several time zones and tens of thousands of square miles, which included hundreds of islands, massive and miniscule, that floated in the azure seas between the warring nations of Japan and the United States.

For its part, the United States was at a staggering disadvantage. The attack on Pearl Harbor had indeed crippled much of its Pacific fleet and nearly all of its air power in Hawaii but, as luck would have it, three of its crucial aircraft carriers were undamaged. As determination would have it, the citizens of the United States quickly rallied around their government and focused intently on the challenge of defeating the Axis powers. In Washington, army and navy commanders decided that the only recourse was to stem Japan's assault from the Pacific quickly, which then might earn the armed forces enough traction to fight in Europe. "All the plan required," dryly stated one naval historian, "was a bigger and better army than the United States or Britain had, a two-ocean navy, supply ships, open supply lines, and bases for planes and supplies." The key to victory in the South Pacific was its islands.

The logistics of an island-by-island offensive were overwhelming. To achieve victory, the Americans would have to move westward in a deadly game of operational hopscotch, nautical mile by nautical mile. The Army Air Corps (there was no Air Force yet) would have to fly reconnaissance sorties to get information about the island in question; photographs would have to be made and accurate information would have to be pieced together from these photos, or old maps, or the recollections of displaced islanders, or some conglomeration of all three. Then, the marines would have to initiate a series of amphibious assaults, followed by enough army troops to secure the island in order to bring in a vast array of medical staff and equipment, supplies, materiel, gasoline, and housing to keep the captured island secure and efficient. The island, now under Allied control, would then serve as a rear guard base for the next operation, stretching ever westward to Tokyo and the eventual victory over Japan. This sequence would have to be repeated over and over again, despite tremendous resistance, in order to succeed. Imagine dropping a crystal vase in the middle of a crowded highway and having to pick up the shards, tiny piece by tiny piece, while passing cars whizzed by lethally in all directions. The challenge was absurd, but it had to be met.

A key piece to this massive logistic puzzle was supplied in the very first week of 1942 by a navy rear admiral named Ben Moreell. Moreell was Chief of the Bureau of Yards and Docks, an engineering division of the Navy that, during peacetime, was mostly involved in reconstructing ports, bridges, and dams in times of emergency. In the months preceding Pearl Harbor, Moreell had foreseen the logistical complexity of a potential war in the Pacific and brought an intriguing solution to the navy brass. The navy could recruit America's most experienced builders and engineers, put them in uniform, and send them overseas to build whatever was needed. This division would be able to turn any jungle island into an efficient base of operations. It could bulldoze palm trees and move hills; it could backhoe raw coral into ravines; it could turn muddy troughs into passable roads; it could assemble harbors out of

mobile pontoons; it could tractor and pave airstrips in the jungle; it could build anything anywhere. The men would also be trained to fight the enemy, if need be—they would certainly need to know how to defend themselves under fire. Moreell's units would be known as the navy's Construction Battalions—or, in the nickname derived from their initials: the Seabees.

The first Seabees were ready to set sail as early as January 27. Known as the "Bobcats," the First Construction Battalion was needed to build a fueling base in Bora Bora, some 2,000 miles south of Hawaii, in order to defend and keep open the sea lanes to Australia. They left the United States in a troop ship with 4,000 soldiers bound for Bora Bora and, upon their arrival, quickly discovered the climatic and logistic disadvantages of a small island. Incessant rainfall, the threat of tropical disease, and a lack of accurate surveys of the island made their task particularly difficult. But the Seabees soon embraced "Can Do!" as their motto and within a few months they had built an airfield, a seaplane base, twelve miles of road, two radio stations, a pier, and a dry dock. According to an Army officer, the Bobcats "smelled like goats, lived like dogs, and worked like horses." The fueling station at Bora Bora had been a key factor in the United States winning its first strategic naval victory over Japan at the Battle of the Coral Sea in early May. The Seabees had earned their stripes.

That military success, along with the United States' naval victory at the Battle of Midway in early June (the American task force destroyed four Japanese carriers), were the first snatches of good news from the South Pacific and they were eagerly welcomed stateside. By this point, James Michener was devouring the newspapers for information about the war. Michener had grown up in Bucks County, Pennsylvania, and was a practicing member of the Society of Friends, or Quakers. They were traditionally opposed to violence of all kinds and, because of their religious beliefs, were actually exempt from military service. But Michener felt that the Axis powers were such a threat to civilization that he was determined to take a leave of absence from his publishing job and enlist.

PREVIOUS PAGE: *The island of Espiritu Santo; Aoba can be glimpsed in the distance.*

PAGE 26: *They're Gonna Wash That Soap Right Outa Their . . . A sextet of ingenious Seabees construct—and enjoy—a group shower on Espiritu Santo, in the New Hebrides Islands.*

OPPOSITE: *A recruiting poster for the U.S. Navy Seabees captures the danger and exoticism of the South Pacific.*

CLOCKWISE FROM TOP LEFT: "Can do!" is the Seabee motto: building wooden water tanks; paving a runway strip; realigning the machine guns of a F4U Corsair; and running a laundry racket—all on the Solomon Islands of the South Pacific.

In his younger days, Michener had traveled as a merchant marine in the Mediterranean and thought his experience might be useful. Twice, during 1942, he traveled to Washington in hopes of securing a commission in the navy but, at the age of thirty-five, he was passed over. In the meantime, his wife Patti, from whom he was becoming increasingly estranged, volunteered for the WACS and moved to Louisiana for training. Michener felt that the head of his local draft board in the city had a grudge against him and was trying to draft him for the army, but Michener trumped him by enlisting for the navy, commission or not. By October, James Michener was ready to fight the war at sea, come hell or high water. Over the next few years, he would encounter a little of both.

Josh Logan was looking forward to his first rehearsal of *By Jupiter* with a mixture of elation and dread—he was eager to be back on Broadway, but concerned that directing a musical might be too stressful for his still healing psyche. But a few weeks before rehearsal began, his apprehensions were upstaged by the United States War Department—he had been drafted. *By Jupiter*'s producer, Dwight Deere Wiman, had other ideas—he needed Logan to fight on West 44th Street. There would be plenty of battles with Ray Bolger ahead, and Richard Rodgers needed reinforcements to get Larry Hart to turn in lyrics. Wiman secured a temporary deferment for Logan and, in the spring of 1942, Logan was attacking the rehearsal schedule for *By Jupiter*.

Putting together a score for the first rehearsal had been a chore for Rodgers. Larry Hart had made himself nearly unavailable for work. One day in February, frustrated by the unreturned messages and phone calls to Hart, Rodgers ventured to Hart's apartment with Hart's doctor in tow. They found Hart lying on his bed in a semistupor and promptly rushed him to a discreet suite in New York's Doctors Hospital. This proved to be a blessing in disguise, as Rodgers simply rented out a hospital room next to Hart's and had a piano installed. Under surveillance, as it were, Hart managed to finish the lyrics over the next few weeks; his doctor discharged him only when the task was complete.

By Jupiter opened on June 3, 1942, one day before the United States Navy achieved its most decisive victory to date at the Battle of Midway. Broadway audiences were eager for the goofy distractions supplied by the musical's mildly titillating hijinks, the buoyant star turn by Ray Bolger and his gravity-defying dances, and, not least of all, Rodgers and Hart's score. *By Jupiter* became Rodgers and Hart's longest running original show, and its 427 performances illuminated a Theater District that was bravely enduring the wartime blackouts of its neon landscape and food rationing in its fancy restaurants and watering holes.

At one of those watering holes, soon after the opening night of *By Jupiter*, a farewell party was being thrown for Josh Logan. He was about to be shipped out for military training at Fort Dix, New Jersey. Logan had a lot on his mind, not the least of which was his imminent divorce from his first wife and a budding romance with an actress named Nedda Harrigan. At the send-off party, Logan spoke to Rodgers about what his next project might be, and he hoped Rodgers might think of him in the future. Rodgers confided that his next project would probably be an adaptation of a somewhat obscure 1931 bucolic play called *Green Grow the Lilacs*, about farmers and cowhands in turn-of-the-century Oklahoma territory. Rodgers had been turning the idea over in his mind since 1940, when he had seen a revival of the play near his country home in Connecticut. There would be just one problem, and it was a major one—the project was not right for Larry Hart. Hart's work habits were simply too maddening to Rodgers and the subject matter was of no interest to him. The idea of Rodgers taking on another partner after two decades of tremendous success with Hart was a frightening one, both to the team and to the theatrical community. Rodgers tentatively asked Logan his opinion of the man he wanted as his new collaborator: Oscar Hammerstein. "Dick," Logan replied, "you and Hammerstein would be unbeatable."

Hammerstein had other things on his mind in the early summer of 1942. For one thing, he was having a thoroughly enjoyable time with his new collaborator—a dead composer named Georges Bizet. Bizet's 1857 opera,

Carmen, had inflamed Hammerstein's imagination years earlier and he had been nursing the idea of an English-language adaptation that would be accessible to Broadway audiences ever since. After the failure of *Sunny River*, he decamped to his Doylestown farm to work on *Carmen*, and he played one 78-rpm record of the score after another, crafting a libretto and lyrics to the music that would replace nineteenth-century Seville with a World War II parachute factory in the South. Hammerstein's adaptation also recast the characters as African Americans, which would require the largest all-black cast seen on Broadway since *Porgy and Bess*. But an actual production of *Carmen Jones*—as it would eventually be called—was a happy abstraction for Hammerstein; for now, this project was for love, or perhaps for therapy. In the meantime, he was heavily involved with the American Theatre Wing War Service, spearheading an entertainment center for servicemen in Times Square, as well as other wartime charitable organizations. Hammerstein was always one of Broadway's most engaged citizens and patriots; even his own son, Billy, had enlisted in the navy.

Several days after he finished his *Carmen* adaptation to his personal satisfaction, Hammerstein received a phone call from Richard Rodgers asking him to lunch in the city to discuss a new project. The phone call was not entirely out of the blue. In September 1941, Rodgers had come calling to the Doylestown farm to sound out Hammerstein about working with him someday, somehow. Rodgers had great respect for Hammerstein; they had known each other since Rodgers was a boy, when his older brother had attended Columbia University with Hammerstein. Hammerstein was one of the best in the business and, better yet, he was a paragon of disciplined craftsmanship and professionalism—the anti-Larry Hart. Since the conversation was strictly theoretical, Hammerstein kept his counsel. He famously advised Rodgers:

> I think you ought to keep working with Larry just so long as he is able to keep working with you. It would kill him if you walked away while he was still able to

function. But if the time ever comes when he cannot function, call me. I'll be there.

By the summer of 1942, that time had come. At their lunch in New York, Rodgers asked Hammerstein if he would be willing to collaborate with him on a new musical for the Theatre Guild. Larry Hart was not interested and had left the country for a vacation in Mexico. Hammerstein was not only familiar with *Green Grow the Lilacs*, he himself had once suggested it to his collaborator Jerome Kern, but Kern was unenthusiastic. "I accept your proposal of marriage," Hammerstein replied, according to Rodgers, who continued, "We hit it off terribly well, we understood each other, I knew what his words meant and I felt I could match them." Throughout the summer, Rodgers and Hammerstein worked on the book and score of their new project.

By the time Rodgers and Hammerstein had finished the first draft of their new show in the first week of August, one of the most important incursions of World War II was taking place half a world away on an island called Guadalcanal. Guadalcanal had been seized by the Japanese in May and it represented their southernmost presence in the Solomon Islands, an island chain of critical importance to the Allies' supply and communications routes. The Allies had managed to decode some of the Japanese transmissions, and it became apparent that the Japanese were building an airstrip at Lunga Point on Guadalcanal. This would be fatal to any Allied presence in the area, so the United States Naval Command decided that Guadalcanal should be invaded and the Japanese airstrip destroyed. It was time to call in the marines—and, not far behind, the Seabees.

Since May, the Seabees had been a presence in another island chain called the New Hebrides, about 500 miles southeast of Guadalcanal. The New Hebrides, with its two main islands, Efaté and Espiritu Santo, had been a kind of gift to the Allies. As a French colony, the New Hebrides could have sided with the Pétain government, which supported the Axis, or with the Free French government in exile. In 1940, they cast their lot with the Free French and the New Hebrides became a loyal base of

THE UNITED STATES NAVAL COMMAND DECIDED THAT
GUADALCANAL SHOULD BE INVADED. IT WAS TIME TO
CALL IN THE MARINES—AND, NOT FAR BEHIND,
THE SEABEES.

operations for the Allies. The larger island of Espiritu Santo was quickly transformed by the Seabees of the Third Construction Battalion into one of the most tactically crucial bases on the planet; within three weeks they had constructed a 6,000-foot airstrip out of virgin jungle. They were soon joined by other Seabee divisions, each with thirty officers and a thousand men, as well as medical officers, nurses, supply officers, cooks, and a chaplain. In addition to the airstrip, the Seabees were able to build—often with damnedest forms of ingenuity—drainage pipes, supply depots, immense fuel supply tanks, washing machines, ice-cream freezers—you name it.

The bases at Espiritu Santo were crucial to the success of the assault on Guadalcanal, providing fuel and airstrips to the planes bombarding the island as well as cover and protection to cargo ships, destroyers, and airplanes in order to keep them out of range of the Japanese bombers. Thanks largely to support from Espiritu Santo, the marines landed successfully on Guadalcanal on August 7. After intense resistance, they were able to take command of the Japanese airstrip the next day. Within weeks, two companies of the Sixth Construction Battalion moved into Guadalcanal and made the airstrip operational. It was redubbed Henderson Field and would prove to be one of the most crucial airfields in the South Pacific.

The Japanese, however, were in no mood to give up complete control of Guadalcanal and sent ships and troops to the island to take it back. The next six months saw some of the most grueling, protracted fighting of the entire war. Still, Seabee battalions were being sent to Guadalcanal, despite constant bombardment from the Japanese, in order to transform the jungle into a base. By Thanksgiving, they had constructed enough freezers for the men to have turkey dinners instead of K-rations. By Christmas, they had built a chapel of coconut logs and palm thatching, where they could congregate and give thanks that—for now, at least—they had survived this part of the war in the South Pacific. The US effort had prevailed—Guadalcanal seemed safely in the hands of the Allies, and the nearby island of Espiritu Santo was operating around the clock as its own small village of American efficiency. After eight months of back-breaking work, valor under fire, and pulling the damnedest rabbits out of their helmets, the Seabees had a hell of a lot of tales to tell.

OPPOSITE: The first wave: a Marine landing on the Solomon Islands.

ABOVE: U.S. Navy nurses were unique among American nurses in that they were given an immediate commission, allowing them to serve as officers, with all the concomitant respect and resources.

FOLLOWING PAGES: Airstrike in the South Pacific, 1943. American forces assault Rabaul Harbour in New Guinea, a Japanese stronghold. A U.S. Army Air Force B-25 swoops down over a Japanese ship, while the coast in the background burns from a heavy bombardment,

SOME ENCHANTED EVENING

Some enchanted evening
You may see a stranger,
You may see a stranger
Across a crowded room.
And somehow you know,
You know even then,
That somewhere you'll see her again
    and again.

Some enchanted evening
Someone may be laughing,
You may hear her laughing
Across a crowded room—
And night after night,
As strange as it seems,
The sound of her laughter will sing in
    your dreams.

Who can explain it?
Who can tell you why?
Fools give you reasons—
Wise men never try.

Some enchanted evening,
When you find your true love,
When you feel her call you
Across a crowded room—
Then fly to her side
And make her your own,
Or all through your life you may dream
    all alone.

Once you have found her,
Never let her go.
Once you have found her,
Never let her go!

Four months before rehearsals were to begin for *South Pacific*, Rodgers and Hammerstein played what had been written so far at a supper party at the Rodgers' apartment. Mary Martin and Ezio Pinza were there (it was the second time they had met), and Martin chimed in whenever one of her songs came up; she already knew them and had no aversion to providing the floor show. Pinza was a different kind of performer altogether; his rule was never to sing in public unless he was prepared and he was paid. He was also not the type to make fawning comments in public and said not a single word after Rodgers played "Some Enchanted Evening." Rodgers looked at him and, in a challenging tone, said, "This is going to be the hit song of the show." Pinza said in his autobiography:

> "It's a very lovely song," I countered. "One of the loveliest I know, but it can't compare in popular appeal with 'A Wonderful Guy.'" Rodgers seemed hurt by my remark, but he has had his sweet revenge.

During Broadway's so-called Golden Age—roughly 1943 to 1964—a musical without a romantic ballad was hardly a musical at all. Among Rodgers and Hammerstein's impressive history of romantic ballads, "Some Enchanted Evening" stands apart from the pack; in fact, it may be the greatest romantic ballad Broadway has ever heard. In the show, "Some Enchanted Evening" comes right out of a very cleverly arranged "duet" between Emile de Becque and Nellie Forbush. Rodgers promised Martin that she would not have to sing at the same time as Pinza, so the two characters' inner thoughts are presented in counterpoint:

> NELLIE
> Wonder how I'd feel,
> Living on a hillside,
> Looking on an ocean,
> Beautiful and still.

> EMILE
> This is what I need,
> This is what I've longed for,
> Someone young and smiling
> Climbing up my hill!

"Twin Soliloquies" had been brilliantly adapted by Hammerstein from some lines of Michener's in the story, "Our Heroine:"

> To herself, [Nellie] was saying, "I shall marry this man. This shall be life from now on. This hillside shall be my home. And in the afternoons, he and I will sit here." Aloud she continued, [The cacao trees] are beautiful, aren't they?
> To himself, De Becque said, "This is what I have been waiting for. All the long years. Who ever thought a fresh, smiling girl like this would climb up my hill. It was worth waiting for. I wonder . . . "

The music that Rodgers wrote was urging and romantic; as he wickedly (and wonderfully) said about "Twin Soliloquies," "Don't tell Kurt Weill, but when I'm supposed to write recitative I write melody instead."

Rodgers was equally skillful in writing the music to "Some Enchanted Evening." Luckily for him, he knew who his Emile was going to be, so the entire musical structure of the song was tailor-made for Pinza's subterranean notes. In 2002, orchestrator and arranger Jonathan Tunick, who had conducted the 1987 CBS recording, explained to interviewer Mark Eden Horowitz:

> Emile's songs are written for a bass, rather than a tenor. His melodies head downwards and land on the tonic, as though they were seeking the earth, just as Emile, the planter, does. He is not only a man of the earth, but one who seeks emotional roots as well, and Rodgers' music brilliantly illustrates this. The psychology of the music is dead-on perfect, and shows what Rodgers could do better than anyone else.

PREVIOUS PAGE: Ezio Pinza shortens the distance of the proverbial crowded room between him and Mary Martin.

OPPOSITE: Richard Rodgers' handwritten manuscript.

"Don't tell Kurt Weill, but when I'm supposed to write recitative I write melody instead." Richard Rodgers

The notes were certainly there when Pinza sang it in rehearsal, but the words were more tenuous. According to cast member Don Fellows, no one could understand what he said: "It sounded like 'some ex-changed an evening.'" When it was explained to Pinza, he said, "I taught I spend-a da night at *your* house, and den you spend-a da night at *mine*."

Once he figured it out, Pinza was eloquently able to evoke the tenderness of Hammerstein's wistful second-person tense—"*You* may see a stranger...Who can tell you why?" Rodgers always had to remind Pinza to finish the "Never let her go" softly the first time around, because when Emile reprises the song at the end of Act One, it is "like carrying a brick behind your back"—*then* the singer can let go with everything he has and bring down the Act One curtain. The story goes that Cole Porter and an acquaintance overheard the song pouring out of the radio one day and his friend remarked what a powerful song it was. "Yes," Porter twinkled in reply, "if you can imagine it taking two men to write one song."

In 1949, that song was pouring out of a lot of radios. Perry Como's version of "Some Enchanted Evening" was Number 1 on the Billboard chart for five straight weeks, and remained on the charts for twenty-six weeks. In addition, renditions by Bing Crosby, Jo Stafford, Frank Sinatra, and Paul Weston made it on the charts—all told, there were six different versions that landed on that year's list of Top 100 recordings. A commercial single of Pinza's rendition from the original cast album even landed on the charts, ranked at number 65 for the year. No matter who else records it, or how well, it will always remains Pinza's signature number, and although he got a little tired of taxi drivers and doormen singing it to him, he was grateful. He fluttered many a heart with his vocal prowess. The secret to his success was put very succinctly by playwright Russel Crouse: "Pinza has three balls and when he sings, they all light up!"

OPPOSITE: Rossano Brazzi tries the same approach with Mitzi Gaynor, from the movie.

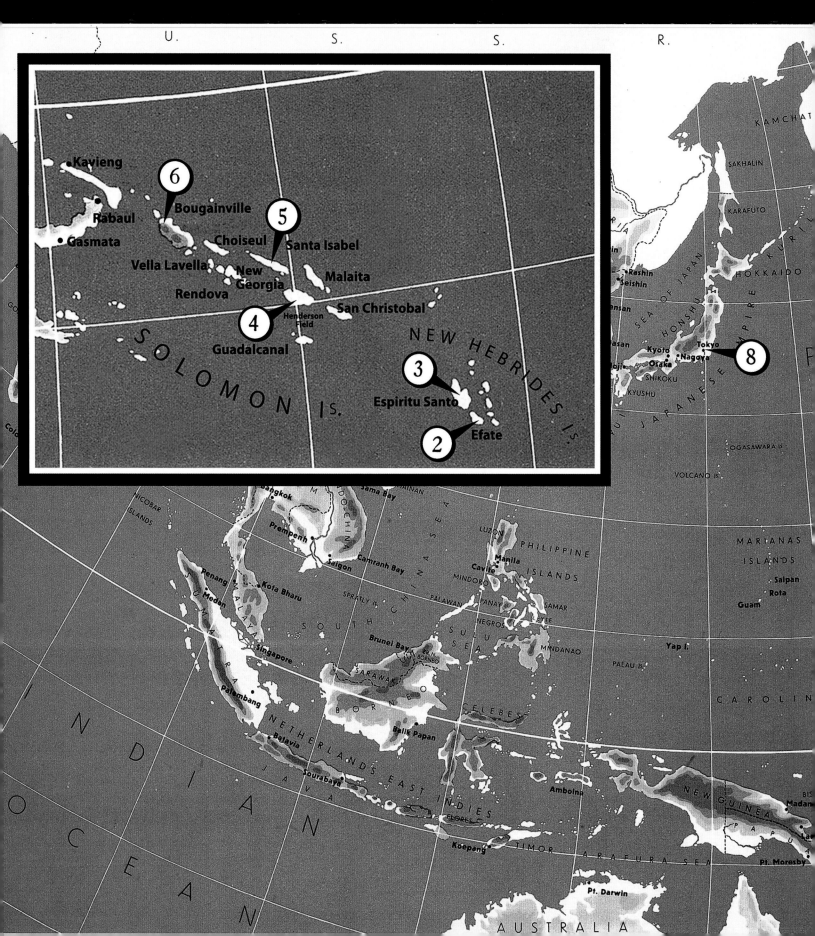

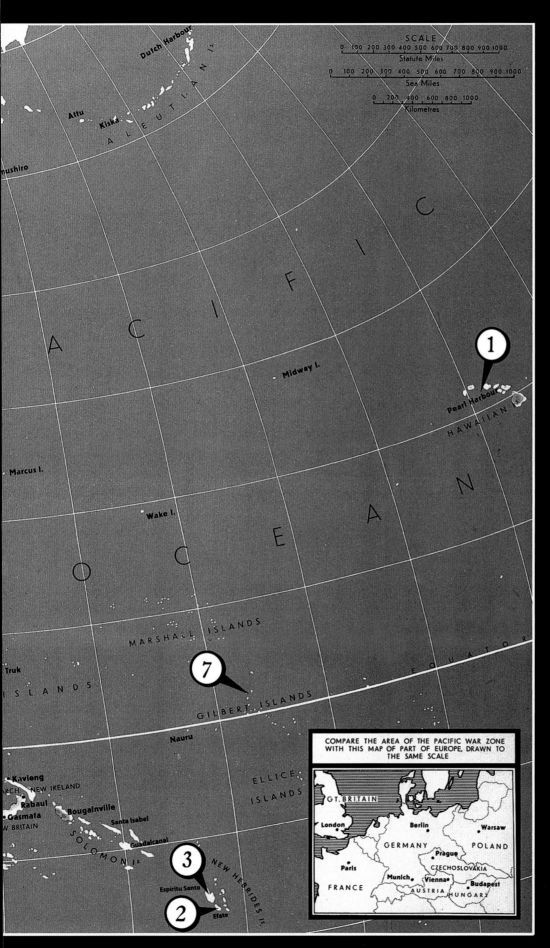

1. Pearl Harbor, Hawaii.
On December 7, 1941, Japanese airborne attack destroys much of America's battleship and air forces.

2. Efaté, of the New Hebrides.
Controlled by the Free French, these islands were secured by the Allies in spring, 1942. In Michener's tales, Nellie Forbush was initially posted here.

3. Espiritu Santo, also of the New Hebrides.
The "site" of *South Pacific* and a major rear-guard and supply base until early 1945.

4. Guadalcanal, one of the Solomon Islands.
The battle to secure this important island lasted from August of 1942 to February, 1943. The Seabees constructed the airstrip on the renamed Henderson Field.

5. Santa Isabel, Solomon Islands.
Bordering "The Slot," a water passageway used by the Japanese to assault American troops on Guadalcanal, this island is probably the basis for "Marie Louise Island," where Cable and De Becque go on their mission.

6. Bougainville, Solomon Islands.
American marine forces capture the island, November, 1943.

7. Tarawa Atoll, the Gilbert Islands.
"Operation Galvanic", the assault force that captures the island, launched in late November, 1943. More than 1,000 American soldiers and nearly 5,000 Japanese are killed within 76 hours.

8. Tokyo, Japan.
6,324 miles from the American mainland. The war against Japan comes to an end on August 15, 1945.

CHAPTER THREE

1943

In the spring of 1943, if you wanted to see the largest congregation of soldiers and sailors in one place on American soil—outside of an army base or training camp—you only had to go to Broadway.

New York's Theater District had become the country's center of entertainment for young men shipping off to the service; indeed, New York's harbor was the country's busiest embarkation point for the armed forces. The servicemen were often given a twenty-four-hour or weekend pass in New York and, smart fellows that they were, they made the most of it. Times Square offered nearly four dozen legitimate theaters (at every musical, the orchestra played "The Star Spangled Banner" at the beginning of the show), almost as many movie theaters (some of which screened a series of features twenty-four hours a day), and hundreds of restaurants, snack bars, and nightspots. The American Theatre Wing had organized the Stage Door Canteen (thanks to the contributions of Oscar Hammerstein, among others), a club open only to servicemen, where they could get a warm meal, a cup of coffee (no liquor allowed), a dance with a pretty girl, and perhaps some improvised entertainment from a Broadway star donating his or her time to provide "something for the boys."

Servicemen could be found onstage, too. *Something for the Boys* was, in fact, the title of a frivolous musical comedy written by Cole Porter; another service comedy called *The Doughgirls* was also delighting audiences. Both of these, however, paled next to the Irving Berlin musical extravaganza that had dominated Broadway six months earlier. *This Is the Army* was not only a vastly entertaining revue of life as experienced by recruits in training camps all over the country, it actually put real servicemen onstage—some 300 of them—and their combined verve, patriotism, good sportsmanship, and talent brought hardened theatergoers to their feet nightly. "That the performers were soldiers made everything better. Many of these same men had performed as civilians to no recognition; now, in khaki, they were budding Chaplins or Carusos. . . . If any show ever took the town, this one did," wrote Josh Logan in his memoirs. Logan would know; while he was in basic training at Fort Dix, a phone call came from Irving Berlin himself. Impressed with Logan's work on *By Jupiter*, Berlin wanted him to take over the directorial reigns of *This Is the Army* during previews. Logan's protestations were futile; Berlin had already arranged with the military brass in Washington for Logan's transfer. Logan's keen eye for the immense logistics of the show was crucial in transforming it from an enthusiastic amateur camp show into a Broadway hit.

However, by April 1943, *This is the Army* had decamped from Broadway and was now touring the country, and Logan had been sent to an Air Corps training base in Miami Beach. Another musical had taken Broadway by storm—the same musical about farmers and cowhands that Rodgers and Hammerstein began working on in the summer of 1942. A great deal had happened since that summer. The Theatre Guild, which was producing the show (called *Away We Go!* because no one could get more enthusiastic over any other title), had an incredibly difficult time raising the money needed to open it on Broadway. Even though Rodgers and Hammerstein were extremely pleased with their work—and their working relationship—and a top-notch production staff and cast had been assembled, the first rehearsal had to be postponed until the early winter of 1943. Rodgers and Hammerstein each had other preoccupations in the meantime: Hammerstein was cautiously negotiating a studio contract with MGM and thinking about how his immense *Carmen Jones* might be staged; Rodgers was applying for a civilian commission in the Air Corps (his daughter, Mary, thought this was quite amusing, as her father had a fear of flying). He was eventually turned down.

By the time their new musical arrived on Broadway on March 31, it had been honed into a carefully crafted, original, striking thing of beauty. Along its tryout journey from New Haven to Boston to Broadway, it had even acquired a new title: *Oklahoma!*. The rejections from the potential producers and investors in the previous months still made the creative team a little nervous, but in a letter to his son Billy, stationed in the South Pacific, Hammerstein expressed confidence: "If [the critics] see that this [show] is different, and higher in its intent, they should rave. I know this is a good show. I cannot believe it will not find a substantial public. There! My neck is out." The critics did, indeed, rave (although, ironically, the *New York Times* critic, Brooks Atkinson, who had been Hammerstein's only relative champion on *Sunny River*, was now serving as a war correspondent; his replacement, Lewis Nichols, raved anyway). *Oklahoma!* became not only the greatest hit of the

war years, but a watershed for the advancement of integral narrative in the American musical. It would go on to run for 2,212 performances, a record for its time.

Of all the upbeat shows on Broadway during the war—and there were many—none of them caught the hearts of American servicemen the way that *Oklahoma!* did. Its pioneer spirit, freshness, and optimism were not only appealing, they were healing. In the words of the show's choreographer, Agnes de Mille, *Oklahoma!* was "a musical about everything we were fighting for." Soldiers and sailors were given free passes to whatever empty seats were available and, since there weren't many of those, they were crammed into the wings by the house management, in defiance of the fire laws for the St. James Theatre. Celeste Holm, an actress who played the show's comic soubrette, Ado Annie, recalled:

> The war was very immediate, very present. Looking down at those khaki uniforms in the audience was very moving. Many people told me it was the last show I saw before I went overseas and it made me prouder to be an American than I had been before—because it really talked about the unselfconscious courage of the people who settled the West.

About the time *Oklahoma!* was going into rehearsal that winter, in the South Pacific, the tides were changing in favor of the Allies. Japanese resistance in Guadalcanal had come to an end when they pulled all their troops out by February 8. It had been a grueling six months; the Americans had lost nearly 1,500 men taking the island, while the Japanese lost 20,000 fighting men, 860 planes, and 24 ships. Soon after, the Seabees completed their usual miraculous transformation of a jungle island into something resembling civilization. One morning on Guadalcanal, Seabee Maintenance Unit 571 invited everyone to the movies that night. There was one tiny problem— Guadalcanal had no movie theater. The unit went to work. "The difficult we do immediately. The impossible takes a little longer," ran a newly adopted Seabee motto. By 7:30pm

PAGE 50: Navy nurses take a break on a tropical beach in the South Pacific.

OPPOSITE, TOP: This is the Army, 1942. Irving Berlin's brainchild, shepherded to success by Josh Logan. Its cast of 300 soldiers was an actual

army unit, Special Services Company #1, and included a regiment of African-Americans, making it the first integrated unit in US Army history.

OPPOSITE, BOTTOM: Oklahoma!, 1943. Rodgers and Hammerstein's brainchild, the great success of the wartime era on Broadway.

1943

ABOVE: Together again for the first time: Hammerstein and Rodgers at an Oklahoma! rehearsal.

there was an outdoor theater, gently sloped to allow every member of the rank and file to view the new movie screen.

Still, even with a movie theater, life on the Solomon Islands was not an easy one. The Solomons are like a loose rope of pearls, strung roughly together in an oval. Guadalcanal is one of the larger islands, at the bottom of the strand, while Bougainville lay several hundred miles diagonally across from Guadalcanal, at the "clasp" of the rope. Bougainville was still held by the Japanese in the spring of 1943, and they frequently used it as a base from which to assault and harass the Allies to the southeast. Planes and ships would travel down the waterway that ran straight through the Solomons, known as The Slot. In June, the Allies decided to move on the offensive and try to capture all the islands northwest through Bougainville with the eventual goal to move even further northwest and neutralize Rabaul, which had been taken from the British early in 1942 and was now a critical island hub of Japanese activity. The massive air and sea assault forces were known as Operation Cartwheel. An island on the "left wing" of the Solomons, Vella Lavella, was captured in August, and Bougainville was successfully invaded after an arduous sea battle on November 1. The Seabees who landed on Bougainville were so good at their job that, at one point, they were repairing an airstrip 700 feet in front of the marines who were supposed to be leading the assault force. Impossible though it may have seemed a year earlier, the Allies were making good progress through the South Pacific; the next step was to bring their assault to the Japanese defense perimeter in the Central Pacific and to start thinking about how to invade the Japanese islands themselves.

The intense action in the Pacific, as well as the war in the European Theater, only increased the desire of young men to serve their country. Josh Logan could have landed a stateside deployment, working in the Office of War Information, but he wanted to see combat. In Miami, he trained to fight for the air corps and studied so assiduously that he was made a squadron commander, and then, an assistant intelligence officer. He applied for a job on a troop carrier unit, whose job would be to drop parachutists into enemy territory in Europe. Logan was accepted and reported to a base camp in North Carolina for further training. As a commissioned officer, Logan had his privileges, including contraband liquor and the occasional visit to New York City, but at least he knew he would not be stuck at a desk job for the duration.

James Michener could only dream of receiving such a commission, with such a unit. In February 1943, he finally made navy lieutenant, junior grade. His age and, even more so, his literary background conspired against him; he was the perfect person to manage bureaucratic material stateside. Michener was sent to Dartmouth, New Hampshire, for special training, then transferred to Washington, and finally sent to Philadelphia, where he was given a desk job as a publications officer in charge of disseminating manuals and booklets. Michener was chaffing to go to war. As he constantly reminded his superiors—or anyone willing to listen—he had served as a merchant marine and sailed in the Mediterranean. Surely, he argued, he could be of use there; after all, there was a lot of action there, too.

Richard Rodgers eventually came to terms with his civilian status. He wrote to Logan about his success with

ABOVE, TOP: Captain Joshua Logan, before his posting to Europe.

ABOVE, BOTTOM: James A. Michener, lieutenant second grade. Both men were eager, willing, and eligible to serve their country.

Oklahoma!: "All of this has been gratifying and I would be a blind fool not to recognize it. It's also fatuous to suppose that a piece of shrapnel in the back of the neck is the only answer to the question 'What did you do in World War II?'" Indeed, Rodgers wrote several wartime morale-booster songs, a few with Hammerstein and several with Larry Hart, who was still Rodgers' "official" songwriting partner. Probably the most well-known of the Rodgers and Hart wartime ditties was a number performed by Ray Bolger for the film *Stage Door Canteen* in June 1943. Dressed as a bumbling air corps cadet, he pokes fun at the nostalgia for homefront sweethearts in "The Girl I Love to Leave Behind":

> If I live through this big romance
> Then the Japs haven't got a chance.
> Her deportment at parties would cause you to weep,
> Lou Costello is slightly more refined.
> While I fight in a tank, on a plane, in a jeep,
> She's the girl I love to leave behind.

It was important for Rodgers to keep working with Hart. Both men knew that Hart could never have collaborated on a show like *Oklahoma!*, but no one could touch Hart's wicked witty way with a lyric. To keep his partnership alive, Rodgers proposed a revival of their 1927 hit, *A Connecticut Yankee*, updating the time-traveling hero to a World War II naval officer. For Hart, the idea of writing a few new songs and retooling some others was something he could be enthusiastic about, and he threw himself into the revival with vigor and relative discipline. Once work on the show was finished, however, Hart lapsed into his old ways. A week before Thanksgiving, *A Connecticut Yankee* opened at the Martin Beck Theatre in New York. Hart was obstreperously drunk on opening night and Rodgers had him evicted from the theater. The next day, Hart had disappeared. Friends found him wandering the Manhattan streets, which had been hit by a blizzard. Within five days of the revival's opening, Lorenz Hart was dead from pneumonia. He passed away in the hospital during an air-raid drill blackout, with Rodgers sitting outside in the corridor.

Oscar Hammerstein, in the meantime, had escaped tragedy and was courting triumph. He had found an enthusiastic producer for his gargantuan *Carmen Jones* in the diminutive Billy Rose. Rose had assembled a huge cast of African-American singing and acting talent, no easy task during an era that did not encourage the theatrical training of blacks, let alone the vehicles in which to feature them. The cast of *Carmen Jones* included singers drawn from every possible daytime occupation, from the police force to the stockyards and the dockyards. The woman playing Carmen was a photo retoucher; another female singer was a receptionist at Random House publishers. The show opened in December only two weeks after *Connecticut Yankee* and was a huge hit. *Carmen Jones* also struck a blow for racial tolerance. No show since Porgy and Bess employed so many black performers so well; it was also one of the few shows to deal, however superficially, with black soldiers during the war. (Ironically, the other show to do so was a serious play, directed by Lee Strasberg, which opened within weeks of *Carmen Jones*. It was about a black serviceman shipwrecked on a Japanese-held tropical island, featured the Broadway debut of Ruby Dee, and ran one week. It was called *South Pacific*.) The critical and popular acclaim for *Carmen Jones* did Hammerstein a world of good, following as it did his success with Rodgers on *Oklahoma!*. Hammerstein looked forward to the New Year with enthusiasm; he had a new partner and new projects could not be far behind.

That Thanksgiving, the major news of the war came from the South Pacific. In Washington, the Joint Chiefs of Staff decided to step up their counteroffensive and move northeast from the South Pacific, attacking Japan from three directions. The Gilbert and Marshall Islands in the Central

OPPOSITE: Luther Saxon and Muriel Rahn, in Hammerstein's Carmen Jones, 1943. Rahn's alternate in the role, Muriel Smith, would play Bloody Mary in the UK version of South Pacific.

ANY SEABEE WHO WAS BORED WITH PLAYING VOLLEYBALL AND PING PONG AND OTHER DANDY GAMES, WAS NOW GOING TO HAVE A CHANCE TO SEE COMBAT. OPERATION GALVANIC WAS THE REAL THING.

Pacific were designated to become the central staging area of the assault. These were difficult islands to take, let alone to hold, so plans detailing the logistics, manpower, and casualty projections were made months in advance in Washington. The plans called for the first major amphibious assault against a heavily defended coast since World War I. The first islands targeted for the assault were Makin and Tarawa; the codename for the assault was Operation Galvanic.

The Commander in Chief of the Pacific Forces, Fleet Admiral Chester Nimitz, assembled a task force from all corners of the South Pacific. It was the largest task force in United States naval history up to that time—eight carriers, seven battleships, ten cruisers and thirty-four destroyers were assembled from Hawaii, Fiji, and the New Hebrides. More than 100,000 marines were brought in, as well as air cover from the Seventh Army Air Force. D-Day was right before Thanksgiving. Any Seabee or marine who had been sitting around on the island of Espiritu Santo for a year and a half, bored with playing volleyball and ping pong and other dandy games, was now going to have a chance to see combat. Operation Galvanic was the real thing.

Sadly, the real thing turned into one of the deadliest incursions of the war. For all the meticulous reconnaissance of Operation Galvanic, several disastrous tactical mistakes were made before the marines hit the beach at Tarawa on November 20. The Japanese had dug in hard, with pillboxes and foxholes made of coconut logs and coral reef; it would take seventy-six hours of continuous shelling from the air and sea, as well as yard-by-yard combat on the ground to dislodge the occupying Japanese army, most of whom had sworn to fight to the death. When it was over, out of 4,700 Japanese on the island, only 100 were taken prisoner—the rest were killed or had killed themselves. One thousand U.S. Marines were killed and more than were 2,000 wounded—numbers similar to the losses suffered at Guadalcanal, but those had taken place over six months. Worst of all, perhaps, was the military's decision to assemble combat footage from Tarawa into a newsreel and screen it for Americans back home. Along with a *Life* magazine pictorial that September, it was the first shocking glimpse that the average citizen had of the devastation and carnage in the South Pacific.

It was in the midst of these events that Captain Joshua Logan, back at Wing Headquarters in North Carolina, was called into the office of his commander, Colonel Julian Chappell. Here it comes, thought Logan, finally a special assignment of import. Indeed it was. Colonel Chappell had a mission for Logan, one that would require his particular experience and skill: could Logan get him house seats for *Oklahoma!*?

OPPOSITE, TOP: Tarawa, the Gilbert Islands. Before Thanksgiving, 1943, Operation Galvanic launched the first incursion into the Central Pacific. The U.S. Marines set up camp at the beach, after storming the island.

OPPOSITE, BOTTOM: Americans back home were shocked by the enormous casualties and brutality of the assault.

THERE IS NOTHIN' LIKE A DAME

We got sunlight on the sand,
We got moonlight on the sea,
We got mangoes and bananas
You can pick right off a tree,
We got volleyball and ping-pong
And a lot of dandy games—
What ain't we got?
We ain't got dames!

We get packages from home,
We get movies, we get shows,
We get speeches from our skipper
And advice from Tokyo Rose,
We get letters doused wit' poifume,
We get dizzy from the smell—
What don't we get?
You know damn well!

We have nothin' to put on a clean white suit for.
What we need is what there ain't no substitute for.

> There is nothin' like a dame—
> Nothin' in the world!
> There is nothin' you can name
> That is anythin' like a dame.

We feel restless,
We feel blue,
We feel lonely and, in brief,
We feel every kind of feelin'
But the feelin' of relief.
We feel hungry as the wolf felt
When he met Red Riding Hood—
What don't we feel?
We don't feel good!

Lots of things in life are beautiful, but, brother,
There is one particular thing that is nothin' whatsoever
in any way, shape, or form like any other.

There is nothin' like a dame—
Nothin' in the world!
There is nothin' you can name
That is anythin' like a dame.

Nothin' else is built the same!
Nothin' in the world
Has a soft and wavy frame
Like the silhouette of a dame.
There is absolutely nothin' like the frame of
a dame!

So suppose a dame ain't bright,
Or completely free from flaws,
Or as faithful as a bird dog,
Or as kind as Santa Claus—
It's a waste of time to worry
Over things that they have not;
Be thankful for
The things they got!

> There is nothin' like a dame—
> Nothin' in the world.
> There is nothin' you can name
> That is anythin' like a dame.

There are no books like a dame
And nothin' looks like a dame.
There are no drinks like a dame
And nothin' thinks like a dame,
Nothin' acts like a dame
Or attracts like a dame.
There ain't a thing that's wrong with any man here
That can't be cured by puttin' him near
A girly, womanly, female, feminine dame!

"Boys in the Navy are boys in the Navy, and there's not much that you can write for them except songs that are fun for them to sing," wrote Richard Rodgers. "With any luck, this makes fun for the audience, too." He would know—as far back as 1928, Rodgers and Hart had written *Present Arms*, a musical set on a Marine base in Hawaii.

Rodgers and Hammerstein's paean to sexual frustration is not only fun and memorable, but its title phrase has entered the language; it is nearly impossible for an actress in England to be made a Dame of the British Empire without a newspaper headline reading "There Is Nothing Like a Dame." Even Mel Brooks makes fun of it in his 2007 musical version of *Young Frankenstein* with the lyric "There is Nothing Like a Brain."

But behind the good-natured humor of the song, there is a good deal of truth. The Seabees and sailors singing the number are, in fact, cut off from the closest source of female pulchritude they can find. As Michener wrote in "Our Heroine:"

> Military custom regarding nurses is most irrational. They are made officers and therefore not permitted to associate with the enlisted men. This means they must find their social life among the officers . . . they find their friendships restricted to men who are surprisingly often married or who are social snobs.

Navy nurses had a much higher profile than army nurses, as they were trained to be medical instructors in addition to their usual duties. They were not permitted on combat lines, but kept on separate cargo ships or stationed in rear-action bases such as the one in *South Pacific*.

Obviously, in a cargo ship or on an island base, a navy nurse would be outnumbered about 200 to 1. As Cole Porter wrote in 1941, "So Near and Yet So Far."

"There is Nothin' Like a Dame" was the first number in the show Josh Logan staged. As he recalled in his memoir, *Josh*:

> I began blocking out "There is Nothin' Like a Dame," and I started pacing as I imagined a caged animal would pace. The men followed me, restlessly pacing back and forth—killing time until the end of the war, till the chance of seeing women again. [I] motioned one man to pace in one direction, another to go the other way, breaking the pattern constantly. Within fifteen or twenty minutes I had staged it.

As Mary Martin told a reporter for *Theater Arts* magazine, "In a minute or two, he had them pacing like hungry lions." The patterns Logan set were so arbitrary, yet so exact, that only the actors knew how to do it; whenever there was a new road company or a replacement in the cast, one of the Seabees would get an extra day's pay for teaching the moves to a new cast member.

Hammerstein wrote a nice couplet that was cut out of town. Perhaps it was just as well, for it might have dated the show, with its reference to a form of microfilmed mail sent to servicemen overseas as a way of saving tons of shipping space for cargo materials—but it is a great line nevertheless, with some clever internal rhymes:

> For a man can't be without a female,
> And the things are few that you can do
> With V-mail.

CHAPTER FOUR

1944–1945

"I dislike seeming to be insubordinate," said James Michener to his superior officer, "but have you read the note at the bottom of my dossier, stating that I have been trained for Mediterranean service?" "You will go to the Pacific!" reiterated the officer. With that, in April 1944, James Michener finally received his marching orders. As fate would have it, his orders would not involve marching, but hours upon hours of flying and sailing. Whether Michener liked his destination or not mattered very little to his superiors—the Navy needed him in the South Pacific.

A week later, Michener set out from San Francisco on the veteran troop ship USNS *Cape Horn*. Michener's ultimate destination was the island of Espiritu Santo in the New Hebrides, but his orders were somewhat ambiguous. A friend had wrangled him an order for a "tour of inspection" of the Solomon and New Hebrides Islands. This made him a kind of ambassador without portfolio and, after he arrived at Luganville Channel on April 21, he began the peripatetic career that would ultimately make him famous around the world. At the time, it seemed like an adventurer's dream—hopscotching the islands of the South Pacific, inspecting installations, delivering dispatches, and supervising transport supplies. It also did not hurt that many officers and functionaries along the way mistook him for a relative of the powerful Vice Admiral Marc A. Mitscher, a fleet air commander in the Solomon Islands. Not a free pass exactly, but the misapprehension helped cut through a lot of red tape.

"I usually got to the islands three days after the fighting was over," recounted Michener humbly. "It was just like going to a Sunday picnic when I landed, and we just walked ashore. I never did anything that a good woman secretary couldn't have done better." He got to know every inch of Espiritu Santo, and became good friends with an erudite French copra planter named Aubert Ratard, who invited him to dinner at his plantation more than a dozen times. Ratard had become vexed with the conduct of some of the Tonkinese workers on his plantation. The French had wrested control of Tonkin from the Chinese in 1885 and it became the northernmost province of their holdings in Indochina. Faced with a lack of experienced workers, the French planters in the South Pacific imported workers from their colony in Tonkin. Under this arrangement, the indentured Tonkinese would work exclusively for

a planter for three years, then take their earnings and their families back to Tonkin and set up enterprises of their own. Among exploitative relationships in the colonies it was better than most but, because of the war, many workers were stranded for years beyond the terms of their agreement. None of Ratard's Tonkinese workers was pleased, but one woman was more obstreperous than the others; she frequently let Ratard know of her displeasure, often threatening to organize the other Tonkinese into some form of resistance. For her revolutionary fervor, she came to be known as Bloody Mary.

Michener was fascinated with such personal details and was so astute at identifying the strange behavior among the various cultures thrown together in the South Pacific that he became one of the navy's most useful trouble–shooters. He could be relied upon to leave his tin Quonset

PAGE 64: Everybody's gotta get into the act; a marine with USO star Patty Thomas, a dancer with Bob Hope's tour in the South Pacific, 1944.

ABOVE: James Michener, bound for the South Pacific, takes a moment of reflection on a transport deck.

OPPOSITE: Captain Josh Logan, center, with members of his Army Intelligence unit. Left of Logan is Robert Preston, 1940s movie star and future Broadway "Music Man."

hut on Espiritu Santo and fly to any one of the dozens of islands in the Pacific to solve some indiscretion or complaint with diplomacy and common sense. On one occasion, Michener was flown to Bora Bora to solve a problem inexplicable to his superiors: a navy man's mother had interceded with her local senator to bring the sailor back from his tour of duty, but the fellow refused to go back to the States, even though he had earned his discharge. Michener discovered that he fallen in love with Terua, a native woman—as many Americans had—and that this woman was pregnant with his child. But paternal sentiment was not the problem. The sailor explained that he was from Alabama and, if he went stateside, his mother would "have to find out sooner or later that Terua was a nigger." Despite his objections, navy rules were navy rules and he was sent back to face the music in Alabama. And, as the incomprehensible traditions of the South Pacific would have it, after the sailor went home, the pregnant Terua was offered to Michener as a gift by her family.

Michener never made any claims for heroics in the South Pacific; he was more than happy to hear the tales of his comrades and cohorts rather than experience them first hand. Indeed, by the end of 1944, most of the action had passed through the South Pacific and was now happening in the Central Pacific. American task forces had not only won back most of the Japanese-conquered islands, they were taking islands that had been part of Japan's empire before the war. The Allies had invaded Saipan, Guam, and the Palau Islands, and General MacArthur had been spectacularly successful in the Battle of Leyte Gulf. The shadow looming over the Americans was the prospect of a ghastly invasion of Japan itself, but even to consider such an immense operation they would have to capture islands such as Okinawa and Iwo Jima in order to build airstrips that could place air power successfully within reach of Tokyo. Those campaigns, along with the recapture of the Philippines, were proposed for 1945.

Still, there was work to do for Michener in the South Pacific, as the American-held islands were important rear-action supply stations and airstrips. Of course, the islands were still the home to numerous American troops, nurses, liaison officers, native islanders and so forth—and wherever there are people, there are problems. Michener described his service in his memoir, *The World is My Home*:

ABOVE: By 1945, Rodgers and Hammerstein were also successful producers. Here they are in their office, writing songs and perusing spread sheets.

OPPOSITE: As part of World War II homefront support, Rodgers and Hammerstein—along with every other major songwriting team—composed a couple of morale boosters: here's one.

This was a real tour involving real islands, people, and incidents. . . . It was exceptional in that it dealt only with the backwaters of war and I was always mindful of the fact that while I was exploring the joyous wonders of Polynesia many of my friends were landing on quite different islands: Tarawa, Saipan, Okinawa. I never forgot that difference.

One night, however, on the Tontouta airstrip on the island of New Caledonia, Michener nearly had his own fatal experience. The pilot of Michener's plane was having difficulty making a landing. By the time the pilot had swooped around the airfield three times, it had gotten dark and visibility was next to nothing. They eventually made a safe landing, but the close shave had a profound effect on Michener. "As the stars came out and I could see the low mountains I had escaped, I swore, 'I'm going to live the rest of my life as if I were a great man. . . . I'm going to concentrate my life on the biggest ideals and ideas I can handle.'" A kind of mid-life battle crisis, a wartime epiphany. Michener made his way back to his Quonset hut in Espiritu Santo, rolled up his sleeves, and started pecking away at the typewriter. "No one knows the Pacific better than I do; no one can tell the story more accurately," he told himself.

From the end of 1944 through the beginning of 1945, Michener spent his free time working on his account of the South Pacific. "Each afternoon, I went up to a deep cacao plantation where I drafted outlines of some stories that had disturbed me," he recalled. "Each night I went to a big empty building with a dozen mosquito bombs and typed up the material I had been thinking about." His only "editor" on the project was a fellow officer, who spent his evenings in the Quonset hut next to Michener's, making jewelry out of exotic shells to sell to the other soldiers. When Michener finished a chapter he would show it to the officer, who would only grunt out a noncommittal "Not bad at all." It was more than enough for Michener, who found his maiden effort at fiction proceeding with an impressive speed and veracity. As he recalled in his memoirs:

> I visualized the aviation scenes in which I had participated, the landing beaches I'd seen, the remote outposts, the exquisite islands with bending palms, and especially the valiant people I had known: the French planters, the Navy nurses, the Tonkinese laborers, the ordinary soldiers and sailors who were doing the work. . . . I wrote primarily for myself, to record the reality of World War II, and for the young men and women who had lived it.

In the early days of 1944, Captain Joshua Logan was given just the kind of military assignment that James Michener had coveted. Logan was being sent as an intelligence officer to England, where he would be essential to the eventual assault on the Nazis. During his service, Logan strained for anonymity, preferring to be "one of the guys," rather than to seek or be given preference for his celebrity status. It did not help that, weeks after Logan landed in England, Irving Berlin had tracked him down and procured a temporary transfer so that Logan could stage the West End version of *This Is the Army*. When he finished that assignment, Logan was stationed on the southeast coast of

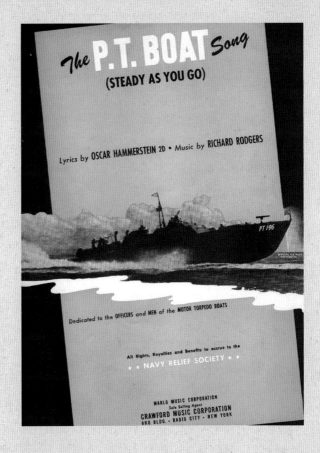

Britain. His job was to brief pilots in the 506th Paratroop Infantry on their role in D-Day. Logan's fighters were to be dropped behind enemy lines at Sainte-Mère-Église, near what would become Utah Beach. Logan's paratroopers were given the go-ahead on June 5, the night before the landing at Normandy. Because of a horrible miscommunication between the pilots and the undercover signalmen on French soil, the paratroopers missed their drop-off point completely; hundreds drowned in the English Channel or were captured by the Germans. Logan was heartbroken and the eventual success of D-Day was of little personal consolation to him.

Logan requested a transfer and took on the kind of assignment that had driven James Michener crazy with boredom—Public Relations Officer for the 405th Fighter Group in Europe. It was a tedious job, requiring him to drum up stories about enlisted men for their local papers stateside— and he enjoyed every second of it. But at the end of 1944, Logan's luck ran out—someone noticed his name on a unit list. He was transferred to the Special Services headquarters in Allied-occupied Paris and put in charge of organizing and staging amateur entertainments for the troops.

Back in the States, Oscar Hammerstein and Richard Rodgers were concentrating on extremely professional

ABOVE: People crowd Times Square at 42nd Street in New York City on May 8, 1945, as the VE Day celebration continues into the night.

OPPOSITE, TOP: The graduation scene from Carousel, which opened on Broadway three week before Victory in Europe. The spirit of a departed father watches over his child—an image that had a profound effect on wartime America.

OPPOSITE, BOTTOM: Oklahoma! meets the South Pacific. A special "tab"— or reduced—version of the show was sponsored as a tour by the USO, which played to millions of GIs in the South Pacific.

productions. *Oklahoma!* continued its successful run through 1944 and beyond. A USO touring version had played in the South Pacific to more than one million home-sick troops. A letter had reportedly arrived at the St. James Theatre requesting tickets for thirteen American service-men; the date was indeterminate, since they were currently prisoners of war in a German stalag. Rodgers and Hammerstein wrote their first (and last) original film score in 1944 for *State Fair*, a glorious piece of homefront cornpone that earned the team an Academy Award for the song "It Might As Well Be Spring." The best part of the assignment for both men was the fact that they never had to be in Hollywood for the filming; *State Fair* was concocted on weekends at their respective country homes in Pennsylvania and Connecticut.

Both men were also busy offstage. Realizing that their theatrical properties were becoming unprecedented successes, they formed a business partnership and a music publishing company. Rodgers and Hammerstein even produced shows they did not write; their maiden attempt, a stage adaptation of *I Remember Mama*, was a tremendous wartime hit. Hammerstein continued his volunteer patriotic duties with such organizations as the Writers' War Board, which was dedicated to promoting freedom and tolerance in America; it led a particular crusade to remove racial stereotypes from American literature and fought for the desegregation of American troops.

It was inevitable that Rodgers and Hammerstein would return to Broadway with a new project. Getting there, however, proved a bit complicated. In November 1944, the head of the Theatre Guild asked the team to adapt another play into a musical, the Hungarian drama *Liliom*, which the Guild had presented to great acclaim in the 1920s. Rodgers and Hammerstein just couldn't see it; the plot centered around a carousel barker, an egotistical bully who brings nothing but unhappiness to his wife and eventually comes back from the dead to chastise his adolescent daughter. As if a wife-beater and the afterlife were not enough, the play's author, Ferenc Molnár, was famously uninterested in anyone touching his original work. Even worse, the show was set outside Budapest, and that was operetta territory, just the kind of thing Hammerstein had written *Oklahoma!* to avoid.

As history confirms, Rodgers and Hammerstein worked through all of those problems and created *Carousel*,

★ 70 ★

a beautifully wrought show, reset in turn-of-the-century New England, enhanced rather than overwhelmed by its inclusion of an existential afterlife. Even Molnár liked it. Of all Rodgers' shows, it was the one that meant the most to him personally, even if he questioned whether audiences would be interested in a musical about faith, which he felt was the essence of *Carousel*. But for an American public that was weary after three and a half years of war, eager for the conflict in Europe to end, and anxious as to whether the conflict in the Pacific ever would end, *Carousel* spoke easily and deeply to its own feelings about faith. As has been pointed out, the hero's brief return from death to observe and inspire his family, who have endured and become stronger in his absence, struck a mightily resonant note with wartime audiences.

Carousel was such a strong piece of theater that it could not be upstaged by the astonishing news that flashed across America three weeks after its opening. On May 8, 1945, the Nazis surrendered to the Allies. V-E Day was celebrated in every street in the country, most noisily in Times Square, around the corner from the Majestic Theatre, where *Carousel* would be happily ensconced for the next two years. Josh Logan celebrated V-E Day while on a reconnaissance mission outside Paris; he had to find some costumes and scenic curtains for a new entertainment he was producing. He was also happily reunited with his romantic interest, Nedda Harrigan, who just so happened to be touring France with the USO. They were in Paris together on August 15, the day the Japanese surrendered.

ABOVE: A sign put up on Tarawa by the Marines, showing their estimate of the length of the war. June 1944. Luckily, the war would be over slightly more than a year later.

OPPOSITE: At Million Dollar Point, rusty remnants of World War II American military equipment lie on the beach and under the waves off the coast of Espiritu Santo Island.

For anyone still fighting in the Pacific or still stuck there maintaining the lifelines to civilization, the victory over Japan was a long-awaited miracle. The carnage that the Army Air Corps brought to Tokyo during the bombing raids in March and the apocalyptic devastation of the two atomic bombs dropped on Hiroshima and Nagasaki were terrible to behold, let alone be responsible for, but every American serviceman in the South Pacific knew that the war would have dragged on for years, and the invasion of Japan was simply too horrific to contemplate.

Sometime between V-E Day and V-J Day, James Michener finished the manuscript of his account of the South Pacific. Since he had spent his civilian life reviewing manuscripts at a New York publishing house, the next step was a foregone conclusion. Afraid that sending his manuscript under his own name to Macmillan would be a conflict of interest, he submitted his manuscript under a pseudonym. Michener wrapped the manuscript in water-proof fabric and sent it via military mail to his former employer. *Tales of the South Pacific*, as it was called, would get to New York a few months before Michener would; he hoped it would crawl its way out of the slush pile before he shipped out. In the meantime, Macmillan had offered Michener his old job as an editor and was eagerly awaiting his return. The firm would have to wait until the end of 1945—the Navy had one last assignment for Michener, as a naval historian. The Navy promoted him to lieutenant commander and gave him the task of preserving the official

history of the islands and cultures he had just spent months recounting in fictional form. Michener took on the assignment, which kept him busy for the last few months of 1945. In the meantime, Macmillan had discovered Michener's ploy in submitting the manuscript. While the senior editors were none too pleased at the deception, they liked Michener's account of the South Pacific. They wanted to publish the stories but, in order to avoid any potential allegation of favoritism for a Macmillan employee, Michener had to agree to revise the material extensively. Unsure as to how to proceed, Michener shelved the manuscript and went about completing his final assignment of World War II.

At the end of the war in the South Pacific, the American navy had no more use for its base in Espiritu Santo. Since it was a French colony, they offered the French all of its military housing, construction equipment, jeeps, supply tanks, and other materiel—for a price. The French countered with an offer that was so ridiculously small that, initiating a new low in Franco-American relations, the navy simply bulldozed everything into the sea outside Luganville Channel and promptly decamped for the States. The natives called their new harbor attraction Million Dollar Point, and it sits there still, forlorn, as one of the great undersea diving attractions in the South Pacific.

As the year ended, James Michener decamped from Espiritu Santo as well, boarding the USS *Kwajalein* for home, with a Million Dollar Idea tucked into his duffel bag.

BALI HA'I

Most people live on a lonely island,
Lost in the middle of a foggy sea.
Most people long for another island,
One where they know they would like to be.

Bali Ha'i
May call you,
Any night,
Any day.
In your heart
You'll hear it call you:
"Come away,
Come away."

Bali Ha'i
Will whisper
On the wind
Of the sea:
"Here am I,
Your special island!
Come to me,
Come to me!"

Your own special hopes,
Your own special dreams,
Bloom on the hillside
And shine in the streams.

If you try,
You'll find me
Where the sky
Meets the sea;

"Here am I,
Your special island!
Come to me,
Come to me!"
Bali Ha'i,
        Bali Ha'i,
                Bali Ha'i.

Someday you'll see me,
Floating in the sunshine,
My head sticking out
From a low-flying cloud;
You'll hear me call you,
Singing through the sunshine,
Sweet and clear as can be:
"Come to me,
Here I am,
Come to me!"

Bali Ha'i
Will whisper
On the wind
Of the sea:
"Here am I,
Your special island!
Come to me,
Come to me."

Bali Ha'i,
        Bali Ha'i,
                Bali Ha'i.

that they serve as the introduction to the musical's overture and set the emotional scene before the curtain even goes up.

Speaking of curtains, the show's designer, Jo Mielziner, knew he would have to paint a scenic drop of Bali Ha'i that measured up to its description and its importance to the plot. After hearing Rodgers' melody, he went back to his studio, picked up his watercolors, and tried to bring Bali Ha'i to life. According to an account of the process that Logan gave to the *New York Times* in 1949:

> The island did not have enough mystery about it, and then, dipping his brush into some water, [Mielziner] blurred the top of this island, making it look as though it were surrounded by mist. This seemed better and he called me. "Come down and look at Bali Ha'i," he said. I called Oscar, who got into a taxi and when he saw Jo's drawing, he thought of an additional lyric for the song.
>
> > Someday you'll see me,
> > Floating in the sunshine,
> > My head sticking out
> > From a low-flying cloud.

Rarely does a song from a musical have such an organic relationship to all its congruent parts. Rodgers was always fond of saying that, in a great musical, the orchestra should sound the way the costumes look. In *South Pacific*, the lyrics sounded the way the scenery looked.

For all its integral specificity to the musical, "Bali Ha'i" had a spectacular life outside of the theater. Perhaps it was born out of the late 1940s/early 1950s fascination with all things tropical and Polynesian—from the restaurant Trader Vic's and the Mai Tai cocktail to the eventual United States statehood of Hawaii—but "Bali Ha'i" was the most commercially successful song from the score, following "Some Enchanted Evening." Perry Como's version was Number One on the Billboard charts for a week, and other versions of the song that landed on 1949's Top 200 included recordings by Bing Crosby, Paul Weston, and Peggy Lee.

Probably the greatest single area of expansion from the stage to movie version was the time spent on Bali Ha'i. Logan constructed Bali H'ai out of various locations, including the island of Kauai, part of the territory of Hawaii. It is a logical decision for a filmmaker to "open up" such a setting, especially when the studio is spending millions on exotic locations.

Now, audiences could see a native Boar's Tooth ceremony, thousands of canoes, grinning villagers, lagoons, and waterfalls. But no matter how attractive Bali Ha'i looks on film—and, unfiltered, it looks damned attractive—Bali Ha'i was never a setting in the first place. It was always a state of mind.

★ 79 ★

ABOVE: Jo Mielziner's stunning watercolor rendering for the original Broadway show, complete with low-flying clouds.

WITH

FRANK
BUTLER

ANNIE
OAKLEY

...LD'S CHAMPION SHARPSHOO...

PART TWO: THE BROADWAY THEATER

CHAPTER FIVE

1946

James Michener and Josh Logan were two of the twelve million who came home. From the middle of 1945 on, servicemen were returning to the United States at the rate of 750,000 per month. The country that they re-entered had changed greatly during the years they were in service. The United States, physically untouched by the war's conflagration, had reaped a surplus of industry and capital that was unthinkable before 1941. Rationing and restrictions were eased, to the relief of everyone who wanted to replace their old car or buy a new set of nylons. During the war, the nation's workforce had added millions of jobs, many filled for the first time by women and African Americans. There would be competition for these jobs, with returning vets entering the ranks of the country's laborers.

A few vets were lucky enough to pick up right where they left off. Logan was to go back into rehearsal for a new Broadway musical—but not just any new Broadway musical. While Logan was abroad in Special Services he had gotten a letter from Richard Rodgers that he and Oscar Hammerstein were about to produce a new show based on the life and sharpshooting adventures of Annie Oakley. It was to star Broadway legend Ethel Merman and was to be written by Dorothy Fields, her brother Herbert, and the composer Jerome Kern.

Kern figured prominently in Hammerstein's plans for 1945 and 1946. Hammerstein wanted to produce a major revival of their *Show Boat*, the show that had revolutionized the American musical in 1927, adding some songs and making some changes. Kern, who had been in ill health in Los Angeles, was eager to come back to New York and plunge into both *Show Boat* and the Annie Oakley musical. Three days after his arrival in the city in November 1945, he was struck with a cerebral hemorrhage and died within the week. Just as Rodgers had lost the major collaborator of his early career, so now did Hammerstein. The *Show Boat* revival opened anyway and was a big hit, but Hammerstein deeply mourned the loss of Kern. Now it was just Rodgers and Hammerstein; they would write musicals exclusively with each other for the rest of their careers.

When Logan arrived at base camp in the States, the first phone call he made was to Rodgers. By this point, Kern had been admitted to the hospital and Logan was devastated to learn that the show he had been hoping for was now in jeopardy. It would be a few weeks before Logan could be officially discharged from the army, due to an eye injury suffered abroad, but by the time he returned to Manhattan and exchanged his khakis for an elegant gray suit, Kern had died and Rodgers and Hammerstein had found a new composer/lyricist for their show: Irving Berlin. (While driving back to the city, Logan heard a new song on the radio and liked it so much, he wanted to sign up the writers; it turned out to be "It Might As Well Be Spring" from *State Fair*. So, in fact, it was Logan who was signed up by the writers, not the other way around.)

For Logan, it was old home week. Not only was he reunited with Rodgers but also with his new friend and champion, Berlin. Hammerstein was new to him, but as a fellow writer, Logan took to him immediately; he once said, "His warmth was so apparent it was hard to see the glints of steel in his eyes." Logan, Rodgers, Hammerstein, and Berlin made a harmonious team (Dorothy Fields, one of the great lyricists of the time, graciously agreed to step aside and only write the book with her brother). *Annie Get Your Gun* opened on Broadway in May 1946 and became one of the classics of the American musical theater. Logan had cemented his relationship with Rodgers and Hammerstein so well that they offered him the directorial reigns on the next show they had lined up for production, a play by Anita Loos called *Happy Birthday*, starring Helen Hayes. Opening on Halloween night, this too was a hit, and featured one of the few non-musical songs ever written by Rodgers and Hammerstein, "I Haven't Got a Worry in the World." When agent-turned-producer Leland Hayward approached Logan at the end of 1946 and offered him the rights to a new romantic comedy called *John Loves Mary*, Logan not only took the directing job but cut Rodgers and Hammerstein in as producers. It would be another smash hit; it looked as if the new team of Rodgers, Hammerstein, and Logan was unbeatable.

While Logan and company were enjoying their Broadway successes, Michener was farther downtown, toiling away. His wartime separation from his wife proved too great; they agreed to divorce soon after his return to the States. Michener spent his days as a senior editor at

PAGE 80: *Broadway bull's-eye! The creative staff and stars of 1946's hit,* Annie Get Your Gun. *From left, rear: Josh Logan, Irving Berlin, Rodgers and Hammerstein, Dorothy and Herbert Fields. Front row is Ray Middleton, who would take over from Ezio Pinza in* South Pacific *four years later, and Ethel Merman, who would simply take over.*

OPPOSITE, TOP: *Fishermen's houses on Espiritu Santo in the New Hebrides.*

OPPOSITE, BOTTOM: *Lieutenant Commander James Michener performs one last task for the US Navy: naval historian. Here, he interviews a serviceman.*

ABOVE: *An islander in Vanuatu, the current name for Espiritu Santo, wears a pig tusk, which has curled into a spiral, around his neck. Pigs, especially their tusks, are highly valued in the New Hebrides.*

ABOVE: A downed Navy pilot in a life raft waiting for the rescue plane in the South Pacific, April 1944.

Macmillan and most of his free time revising his manuscript, which, in turn, was being edited by his own colleagues at Macmillan. In early spring, the publisher felt confident enough in the revisions to offer Michener a contract. He accepted, and *Tales of the South Pacific* was put on Macmillan's fall list.

Although it has always been referred to as a collection of short stories, that is not truly accurate. *Tales* is, indeed, composed of nineteen short stories, but there is a subtle narrative connection among them. A narrator introduces the reader to the world of the American occupation of the South Pacific during the years 1941 to 1943; this narrator seems to hold the same sort of military appointment as Michener's, but the details of his duties are unclear and the point of view shifts frequently. Characters appear in one story and then disappear in the next, only to re-emerge in later stories and in different places. All of the plotlines in *Tales*, however vaguely related, culminate in "Operation Alligator," the story of the immense military assault on a Japanese-held island that serves as the book's climax. In this way, Michener anticipates the kind of multi-level storytelling, in which many different story lines and characters are inter-woven, that are found in late twentieth-century film–making, in movies such as *Pulp Fiction*, *Traffic*, or *Syriana*. At the same time, Michener plays out his incidents and characters against a broad historical canvas, much like an Edna Ferber novel or the film of *Titanic*, for that matter. Somewhat frustrating for the literary or historical critic is Michener's propensity for fictionalizing some places and people—for dubious reasons of military discretion—while keeping others historically accurate: Operation Alligator on Michener's island of Kuralei is, in reality, an account of

Operation Galvanic, the military assault on Tarawa, a fact that may not be readily apparent to the casual reader.

The tales begin with "The South Pacific," a brief elegy for the people of the islands and the beauty of the landscape, a kind of overture to the panorama that awaits the reader:

> Our war was waiting. You rotted on New Caledonia waiting for Guadalcanal. Then you sweated twenty pounds away in Guadal waiting for Bougainville. There were battles of course. But they were flaming things of the bitter moment.

The cast of characters enter with the next story, "Coral Sea," which introduces a group of isolated Allied airmen and a stranded New Zealander during the Battle of the Coral Sea. The first major recurring character is the raffish Tony Fry, an American officer with a propensity for going off the ranch. He appears in "Mutiny," in which he refuses to follow orders to blast away a local island monument to make way for an American airstrip.

In "An Officer and a Gentleman," Ensign Bill Harbison, an ambitious married officer, is sent to the small island of Efate. The grind and boredom wear him down and he seeks affairs with various Navy nurses on the island, including one named Nellie Forbush:

> [She] was a slender, pretty nurse of twenty-two. She came from a small town in Arkansas and loved being in the Navy. Never in a hundred years would Bill Harbison have noticed her in the States. . . . But on the island of Efate where white women were the exception and pretty white women rarities, Nellie Forbush was a queen. She suffered no social distinctions.

Nellie falls in love with Harbison, who withholds his married status from her. One night, in his cups, he tries to rape Nellie, but she resists and he throws her over, far too concerned with his image to connect truly with anyone else.

One of the most harrowing stories is "The Cave," in which a group of servicemen are stationed in a cave on a small island, trying to prevent the Japanese from recapturing Guadalcanal. Tony Fry reappears; his mission is to receive radio transmissions from a fellow they call the Remittance Man, a name borrowed from Mark Twain, referring to someone who was paid by his family to travel the world rather than remain at home. The Remittance Man turns out to be Anderson, a local British trader who has risked his life to hide out on nearby Santa Ysabel island in the Solomons and secretly broadcast Japanese troop movements to the Allies. For weeks he begins each broadcast with a local weather report, then the Japanese troop movements down the Slot, and concludes each transmission with "Good hunting, Americans!" At one point, he goes completely undercover for fear that he has been discovered. Weeks later, after the Japanese troops depart from Guadalcanal, Fry and the servicemen from the cave demand of their superior officer that they send a rescue party to find the Remittance Man. The commander accedes to the request, but the servicemen discover that the Remittance Man and his confederates had been brutally murdered by the Japanese before their retreat.

In "The Milk Run," Lieutenant Bus Adams, a naval bomber pilot, is shot down in the Pacific without even a life raft. His rescue becomes a matter of honor with the Navy and they do everything in their power to get him back. They succeed, but the naval action winds up costing the American taxpayers $600,000: "But," observes the narrator, "it's worth every cent of the money. If you happen to be that pilot." Michener then moves on to "Alligator," a story which has no characters, only the details of the tremendous logistics required to attack the island of Kuralei (Tarawa), details which stretch backwards months to the Joint Chiefs of Staff in Washington, D.C.

Nellie Forbush reappears in "Our Heroine." The narrator tells us she is from "Otolousa"—Michener's pseudonym for Little Rock, Arkansas—and she has been transferred from Efate to Espiritu Santo. She is among a small group of nurses and officers who are invited to dinner at the plantation of a sophisticated Frenchman named Emile De Becque:

> [He] was a remarkable fellow. He was in his middle forties, slim, a bit stoop shouldered. His eyes were black and deep-set. His eyebrows were bushy. He had long arms and wrists, and although he used his hands constantly in making conversation, they were relaxed and delicate in their movements. . . . The tall Frenchman was eager for someone to talk to,

I'M GONNA WASH THAT MAN RIGHT OUTA MY HAIR

NELLIE
I'm gonna wash that man right outa my hair,
I'm gonna wash that man right outa my hair,
I'm gonna wash that man right outa my hair,
And send him on his way!
Get the picture?

NELLIE AND GIRLS
I'm gonna wave that man right outa my arms,
I'm gonna wave that man right outa my arms,
I'm gonna wave that man right outa my arms,
And send him on his way!

Don't try to patch it up—

GIRLS
Tear it up, tear it up!

NELLIE
Wash him out, dry him out—

GIRLS
Push him out, fly him out!

NELLIE
Cancel him and let him go—

GIRLS
Yea, sister!

NELLIE
I'm gonna wash that man right outa my hair,
I'm gonna wash that man right outa my hair,
I'm gonna wash that man right outa my hair,
And send him on his way!

If the man don't understand you,
If you fly on separate beams,
Waste no time!
Make a change,
Ride that man right off your range,
Rub him outa the roll call
And drum him outa your dreams!

GIRLS
Oh-ho!
If you laugh at different comics,
If you root for different teams,
Waste no time,
Weep no more,
Show him what the door is for!

Rub him outa the roll call
And drum him outa your dreams!

NELLIE
You can't light a fire when the wood's all wet,

GIRLS
No!

NELLIE
You can't make a butterfly strong,

GIRLS
Uh-uh!

NELLIE
You can't fix an egg when it ain't quite good,

GIRLS
And you can't fix a man when he's wrong!

NELLIE
You can't put back a petal when it falls from a flower,
Or sweeten up a feller when he starts turning sour—

GIRLS
Oh no, oh no!

NELLIE AND GIRLS
If his eyes get dull and fishy
When you look for glints and gleams,
Waste no time,
Make a switch,
Drop him in the nearest ditch!
Rub him outa the roll call
And drum him outa your dreams!
Oh-ho! Oh-ho!

I went and washed that man right outa my hair,
I went and washed that man right outa my hair,
I went and washed that man right outa my hair,
And sent him on his way!

GIRLS
She went and washed that man right outa her hair,
She went and washed that man right outa her hair,
She went and washed that man right outa her hair,

NELLIE AND GIRLS
And sent him on his way!

ABOVE: *The moment that eventually stopped the show—the bubbly Martin.*

PAGE 89: Mary Martin, in a posed color set-up, washes her hair one extra time—number 862?

PAGES 90–91: Mitzi Gaynor does her bit to fight dandruff on the shores of Kauai in the movie version.

OPPOSITE: *Don't Rain on My Pomade: After the final performance of South Pacific on January 16, 1954, the creators of the show put three of their Nellies through the rinse cycle, one more time. Mary Martin, left; National Tour star Janet Blair, center; and Martin's replacement, Martha Wright, right.*

Mary Martin was not just naked; according to her, she was "stark, stark, stark naked." She had an idea while in the shower and immediately ran out to tell her husband. It had occurred to her that she had never seen anyone sing on stage while they were washing their hair, which of course in real life, people do all the time. Her husband cautioned her to keep the idea to herself; after all, did she really want to wash her hair six nights a week, twice on matinee days? Martin called Josh Logan anyway and told him her idea. "Don't say another word," he replied. "I've got to call Dick and Oscar!"

Rodgers quickly came up with a tune for "I'm Gonna Wash That Man Right Outa My Hair," and Logan decided to stage it around a jerry-built outdoor shower he remembered from the army. Jo Mielziner designed it to Logan's specifications. Everyone thought the number was going to bring down the house, but when the show played its first tryout performance in New Haven, Logan was horrified to see that the audience barely acknowledged the song, let alone Martin's gamine shampoo specialty. He could not figure out what went wrong until a friend pointed out that the minute Martin started lathering up—live, on-stage—everyone in the audience started nudging each other and admiring the cleverness of the staging. No one had bothered to listen to the song.

The next night, Logan moved the actual shampooing until later in the song, after Martin performed a verse or two of it. Her actual "washing out" was underscored by some of Rodgers' most amusing music in the show—a jitterbug danced by the other Navy nurses, as if they had just cranked up the radio. After Logan made the change, Martin stopped the show nightly—and wound up washing her hair 861 times during the run of the show. Talk about working yourself into a lather!

TALES OF THE
South Pacific

James A. Michener

CHAPTER SIX
1947

T he old adage, "You can't judge a book by its cover," would have been emphatically embraced by James Michener.

When Macmillan finally released *Tales of the South Pacific* in February, the inside text was, in the words of its author, "one of the ugliest books published that year or in any other year." In order to use up their wartime-restriction paper stock, Macmillan printed the book on a thin, dirty-brown colored paper; and, to save money, the stories were run one after another with no page break between them. The book's physical appearance cut the meticulous Michener (who took pride in the books he edited) to the quick: "It was an ugly, monstrous book, a disgrace to a self-respecting company and a humiliation to its author."

Luckily the press could see beyond its cosmetic defects. In the Sunday edition of the *New York Times*, reviewer David Dempsey called it, "truly one of the most remarkable books to come out of the war in a long time. . . . The book's only weakness—the interminable length of some of the tales. Mr. Michener saw so much, and his material is so rich, that he simply could not leave anything out." The daily *Times* reviewer, Orville Prescott, praised the book both in the *Times* and, later, in the *Yale Review*: "Mr. Michener . . . is certainly one of the ablest and one of the most original writers to appear on the American literary scene in a long time." The book sold fairly well. "It enjoyed a faltering life of about five weeks," recounted Michener in his memoir, "but in that brief period, it proved that a book does not have to garner a huge audience in order to succeed ultimately." Macmillan seemed pleased; there had been some concern that *Tales* would be subsumed by another collection of short stories about navy life in the South Pacific that had been released in 1946: *Mister Roberts*, by a young naval vet named Thomas Heggen.

Josh Logan had been given *Mister Roberts* by an agent friend of his, and took it with him to Cuba, on a honeymoon "brush-up" with his new wife, Nedda Harrigan. He found much to enjoy in it. Heggen's book went beyond, or rather beneath, the kind of wartime heroics found in most magazines and novels of the time. Just like Michener, his theater of operations was the South Pacific (Heggen had seen active duty on Okinawa and Iwo Jima) and he also focused on the average guy who was waiting for orders and waiting out the war. In fact, the book was, in Heggen's words, a tale "from apathy to tedium with occasional sidetrips to monotony and ennui." The eponymous Mister Roberts, a lieutenant junior grade (just as Michener was when he went to the South Pacific), is a college man stuck on a Navy cargo ship but itching to prove himself in combat. He and his crew are driven to distraction by their petty, tyrannical captain. Mr. Roberts' selfless attempts to gain some decent privileges for his crew makes him a hero in their eyes; when he eventually dies in combat, his spirit inspires his devastated crew to fight the captain and demand the respect they deserve.

Heggen's book—again, like Michener's—was composed of too many small narratives to add up to one great structural story, but the character of Roberts was so compelling and the ironic detail of a serviceman's life rendered so accurately that it seemed a natural for some more expansive form of dramatic retelling. Logan toyed with the idea of adapting *Mister Roberts* into a play, but another script arrived in the mail, sent by producer Irene Mayer Selznick, that commanded all his immediate attention: *A Streetcar Named Desire*. Tennessee Williams' latest play was being offered to Logan and he devoured every word of it. He knew that directing it would change his career. Unfortunately for Logan, but probably to the good of American theatrical history, Williams insisted that Elia Kazan direct the play instead, and Logan was denied one of the great dramatic breakthroughs of the twentieth century. The second blow came when a friend informed him that *Mister Roberts* had been optioned by another producer and that Heggen and another playwright were adapting it for the stage.

Luckily that other producer was Leland Hayward, the same agent-turned-producer who had let Logan in on *John Loves Mary*. Hayward had an uncanny theatrical instinct (he had also just produced *A Bell for Adano*, a successful play set in wartime Italy) and he was more than happy for Logan to join the new project. But for the moment, although Logan could coproduce and direct the play, it was still Heggen's script. Logan would have to read it and decide how to negotiate a collaboration with Heggen. Heggen's draft definitely needed work—it was too episodic and without a dramatic structure—and Logan convinced Heggen to join him at his Connecticut home and work with him on the script. For months, the two men collaborated and what emerged—once Logan got Heggen to agree to share coauthor credit with him—was a harmonious partnership and a whopping good play. Hayward was ecstatic and plans were quickly drawn up to get *Mister Roberts* on the boards.

In the meantime, Rodgers and Hammerstein were itching to get back on the boards themselves. They had nothing but theatrical successes since *Carousel*—but those were as producers. Rodgers and Hammerstein produced shows well, but they did something else even better: write them. Their next project was to be original, in every sense of the word. *Allegro*, as the show was eventually called, was Hammerstein's idea. It was the story of Joseph Taylor, Jr., a contemporary American from a small town, told from the moment of his birth through his maturity—"his mental maturity that is; and when Joe reaches this point he turns his back on the easy and hollow success he has had and aims for a life of more solid satisfaction," in the words of anthologist Burns Mantle. On the surface, the story seemed a rehash of the old gain-the-world-and-lose-your-soul morality tale but, as Hammerstein said, "If men are continuing to squander their time and usefulness for the wrong things, it would seem important to point this out to them."

What made *Allegro* so compelling, and so indicative of the theatrical courage of Rodgers and Hammerstein, was its presentation. Inspired, no doubt, by the simple metaphysics of Thornton Wilder's *Our Town*, Hammerstein

PAGE 94: *The cover of the first edition of Tales of the South Pacific. Although the illustration barely captures the majesty of the actual location, to Michener, it was far preferable to the "disgraceful" printing of the text inside.*

OPPOSITE, TOP: *Rodgers and Hammerstein, in Boston's Public Gardens in*

September 1947; *perhaps they are reading the reviews of their Allegro, which was trying out in Boston at the time. If so, they are putting on their game faces.*

OPPOSITE, BOTTOM: *The large cast, allegorical chorus, and minimal scenery of Allegro.*

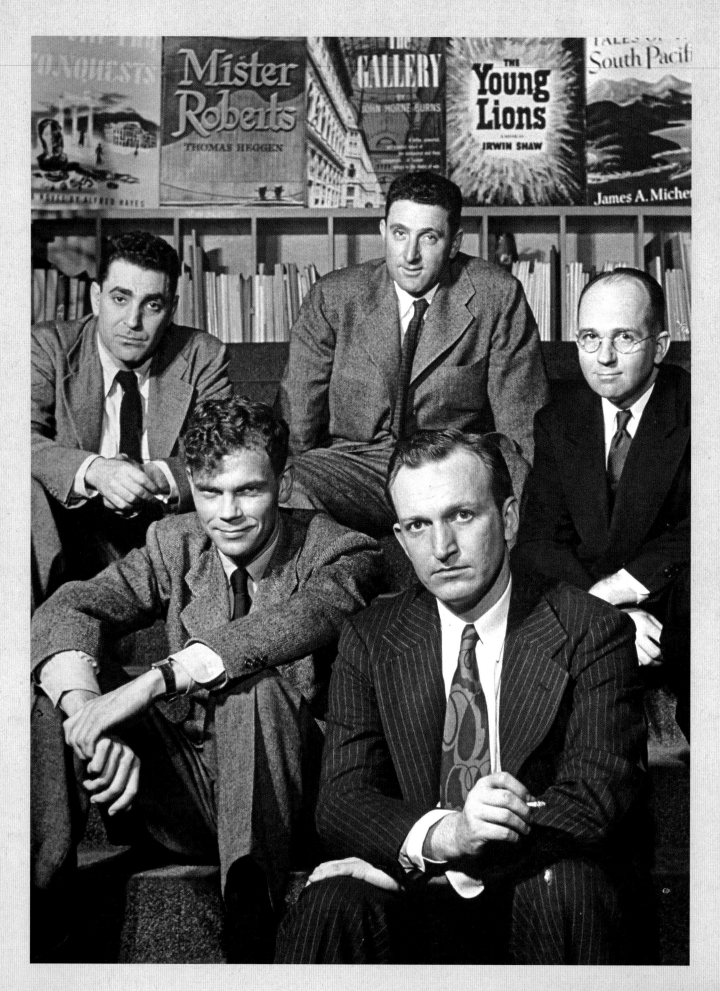

stripped *Allegro* down to its core. There were few props. The scenery was sparse but evocative, using rear-screen projections and drapes that would "wipe" the many locations from one to another quickly, as in a movie. A contemporary chorus functioned as Joe's psyche, voicing (usually in song) his inner thoughts. The staging of the musical would require a particularly sensitive integration of movement and transitions, of sound and light, and Rodgers and Hammerstein turned, not to Joshua Logan, but to the choreographer Agnes de Mille, who had worked wonders on *Oklahoma!* and *Carousel*. As director and choreographer, de Mille would have a huge and unprecedented task ahead of her; she was ably abetted by the stage designer Jo Mielziner, the current design superstar of the American theater.

While Rodgers and Hammerstein were writing the script and songs for *Allegro* at Rodgers' house in Connecticut, they attended a weekend party with their wives. Among the guests were the Broadway musical comedy star Mary Martin and her husband Richard Halliday. As a "party piece," Martin sang her own powerful rendition of "You Can't Get a Man with a Gun," the comic highlight of *Annie Get Your Gun*. By all accounts, she blew the coffee cups and dessert plates off everyone's laps—and was consequently offered the London production of *Annie Get Your Gun*. She preferred to head the national tour instead and asked for Logan, whom she had never met. Logan took a break from his playwriting chores with Tom Heggen to recraft Annie's style from Ethel Merman's delivery to the very different approach of Mary Martin; the tour was set to start in the winter, beginning in Dallas, near Martin's hometown.

In September, Logan also took another break to travel to New Haven and take a look at *Allegro*'s out-of-town tryout. By now, *Allegro* had been nearly crushed by its own ambitions. The cast was enormous, the scenery

mechanically complicated, the story overwhelming. Hammerstein had been forced into helping de Mille with the staging of the dramatic scenes. Logan admired much of it, but sent Hammerstein pages and pages of notes, begging him to refocus the action, fire some of the cast, and cut several of the numbers. Hammerstein resisted most of Logan's suggestions and the show lumbered on to Boston, then New York's Majestic Theatre on October 10, where it ran for nearly a year. The critics were divided; some thought that *Allegro* was revolutionary and inspiring while others found it sententious and predictable. Although a one-year run was not bad, and the show yielded a hit song or two, it was not enough for Rodgers and Hammerstein. Rodgers always felt the show was "preachy" and it did not occasion his best work, but for Hammerstein the relative failure of *Allegro* was to gnaw at him for the rest of his life. He, more than anyone of his generation, had always envisioned the musical stage as a place to challenge the audience and inter- ject a serious, thoughtful note; now he had to wonder if he had misjudged the public, or worse, his own talent.

Michener knew, as Hammerstein surely did, that the only thing an author can do, success or failure, is to get back to the typewriter. In between going to work at Macmillan and reading his reviews for *Tales of the South Pacific*, Michener was starting on a new book, a fictionalized version of his early life in Bucks County, eventually titled *The Fires of Spring*. By the fall, he was beginning to see some royalty payments from *Tales* and the news from California—that *Tales* had been rejected by the script department at MGM Studios as having "no dramatic possibilities whatever"— made little impression on him. Although he had not even finished his second novel, Michener felt instinctively that a writer writes for his own satisfaction, not for fame or financial gain.

OPPOSITE: Five new authors of 1947: Alfred Hayes, Irwin Shaw, James A. Michener, top row, and Thomas Heggen and John Horn Burns, bottom row, framed by enlarged cover of their books.

ABOVE: Thomas Heggen and Josh Logan prepare for the stage version of Mister Roberts. Although Heggen and Michener started at the same time, with similar material, Heggen deeply resented Logan and Michener's success on South Pacific. Heggen himself would burn out quickly and commit suicide in 1949; his abuse of his talents served as a cautionary tale to the disciplined Michener.

By the beginning of December, Logan had been pushing along with his next project. *Mister Roberts* had been cast with the redoubtable Henry Fonda as the lead, and Hayward was preparing for a Broadway opening in February 1948. Rehearsals were about to begin when Logan and his wife went to the December 3 opening of *A Streetcar Named Desire*, as guests of the play's designer, Jo Mielziner, the same designer who had worked on *Allegro*, and who was about to design *Mister Roberts*. Whatever rancor Logan felt about being passed over for the play was offset by *Streetcar*'s genius and, even more so, by the fact that Logan was about to go into a rehearsal for a show that smelled like a big hit.

After the show, the Logans celebrated with Mielziner and the cast and crew at Sardi's, Broadway's legendary watering hole. Logan was introduced to Mielziner's half-brother, Kenneth MacKenna, who happened to be the head of MGM's literary division. When MacKenna was told about Logan's new project, he recommended a book he had just finished reading. "This is a book that's been going the rounds in Hollywood, but every story department has refused it because they felt that war stories were overdone," MacKenna told Logan. As Logan recounted to a 20th Century Fox publicist in 1957, "Kenneth suggested I read the book just because he thought it might give me some insight into the war [in the South Pacific]." Logan hardly thought he needed any deeper insight into a war he had fought but, as he was on his way to Florida for a little R and R before rehearsals for *Mister Roberts*, he chucked a copy of *Tales of the South Pacific* into his suitcase.

As fate would have it, Leland Hayward accompanied Logan to Miami Beach for a vacation of his own. He asked his traveling companion just what the book was that Logan had been devouring so avidly on the plane ride down. Eager not to lose this property as well, Logan hemmed and hawed but, the next morning, he discovered that Hayward had stolen the book from him and had ploughed through it. Hayward concurred with his producing partner—*Tales of the South Pacific* was great stuff. Logan opined that it would make a terrific musical, especially if the score were written by Rodgers and Hammerstein. "Of course, but don't you dare mention it to them," Hayward told Logan, knowing full well of Rodgers and Hammerstein's producing prowess. "They'll want the whole goddamn thing. They'll gobble us up for breakfast." The story that excited them Logan and Heyward most was "Fo' Dolla'" because, as Logan said, "it had some of the tragedy of *Madame Butterfly*." They set about discreetly getting the rights to the story from James Michener.

However, as Logan would have been the first to admit, "discreet" was not in his nature and barely in his vocabulary. Back in New York, shortly before Christmas, Logan met Rodgers at a cocktail party. Rodgers told him that he and Hammerstein were casting about for a good new musical subject. Logan let it slip: "Don't tell anyone I told you this, but I own a story you might make a musical of." Rodgers pulled out his omnipresent notebook and jotted down the cryptic code: "Get Fo Dolla, T of the SP."

"DON'T TELL ANYONE I TOLD YOU THIS, BUT I OWN A STORY YOU MIGHT MAKE A MUSICAL OF."
JOSHUA LOGAN

A WONDERFUL GUY

I expect every one
Of my crowd to make fun
Of my proud protestations of faith in romance,
And they'll say I'm naïve
As a babe to believe
Any fable I hear from a person in pants.

Fearlessly I'll face them and argue their doubts away.
Loudly I'll sing about flowers and spring.
Flatly I'll stand on my little flat feet and say,
Love is a grand and a beautiful thing!
I'm not ashamed to reveal
The world-famous feeling I feel.

I'm as corny as Kansas in August,
I'm as normal as blueberry pie.
No more a smart
Little girl with no heart,
I have found me a wonderful guy.
I am in a conventional dither
With a conventional star in my eye,
And you will note
There's a lump in my throat
When I speak of that wonderful guy.

I'm as trite and as gay
As a daisy in May,
A cliché coming true!
I'm bromidic and bright
As a moon-happy night
Pouring light on the dew.
I'm as corny as Kansas in August,
High as a flag on the Fourth of July!
If you'll excuse
An expression I use,
I'm in love,
　　　I'm in love,
　　　　　I'm in love,
　　　　　　　I'm in love,
I'm in love with a wonderful guy!

"I SANG IT AND I SANG IT AT THE TOP OF MY VOICE, ESPECIALLY AT THE END. AND WHEN I FINISHED, I FELL OFF THE PIANO BENCH!"
MARY MARTIN

"The first night we ever heard 'I'm in Love with a Wonderful Guy,' we were in Josh Logan's apartment in New York and Dick Rodgers called me and said, 'Come over,'" Mary Martin told a BBC reporter in 1968. "When I arrived, he said, 'I have a song—I have *the* song for you.' It was about midnight and Dick, who has the most divine rhythm, the most *perfect* rhythm, played it for Oscar, who sang it in his darling, darling voice. After I heard it played through once I said, 'Could I have the lyrics, could I look at it, and could I sing it—now.' So I sat down beside Dick and he played it and I sang it. I sang it and I sang it at the top of my voice, especially at the end. And when I finished, I fell off the piano bench! And Richard Rodgers turned to me and looked at me on the floor and he said, 'Never sing it any other way.' Then the telephone rang and the manager said, 'You are disturbing the neighbors around you in the apartment house. Please keep it down!' Dick turned to Oscar and said, 'Wait until they have to pay who knows how much to hear this song sung!' Which they did!"

One day, during one of the final run-throughs before *South Pacific* left for New Haven, Martin had an idea for the end of the song; as the traveler curtain closed behind her, she could still sing the song and, in her jubilation, turn cartwheels. Josh Logan thought it was a fine idea and she gave it a try, as the arranger Trude Rittmann continued on the piano in the orchestra pit. But Martin had lost her sense of direction and, in an instant, cartwheeled not across the stage but right into the pit, hitting the piano and knocking Rittman unconscious. Both she and Rittmann were gently brought out of the pit; Martin had bruised her ribs. Some members of the cast thought this was going to mean the cancellation of the show.

Thankfully, both ladies recovered the next day. Martin was bruised black-and-blue all over her side, but, being the good sport she was, the star brought in a football helmet covered with flowers as a gift for Rittmann. The show moved uneventfully to New Haven. As Logan wrote, "We settled for a good safe high note."

PAGE 103: Mitzi Gaynor celebrates her guy; Josh Logan repeated his effective use of an overturned boat in the staging of the film.

OPPOSITE: Mary Martin is a similar situation in the West End production, 1951.

CHAPTER SEVEN
1948

ister Roberts had one of its pre-Broadway tryouts in Philadelphia in late January and, in order to return Josh Logan's favor on *Allegro*, Oscar Hammerstein ventured forth from his country house in nearby Doylestown to give notes on Logan's show. He had very few comments; *Mister Roberts* was a smash from the get-go, and audiences—somewhat weary of the insistent rah-rah boosterism of most movies about World War II—reveled in the more realistic depiction of the war. Veterans who caught the show thought it had perfectly captured the capriciousness and tedium of military service.

After making some minor obligatory suggestions, Hammerstein turned the conversation back to himself; he and Rodgers were having difficulties finding a new show. Logan was surprised—had Rodgers not told him about "T of the SP"? He had not. Logan told Hammerstein to get a copy immediately. Hammerstein read the book and called Logan two days later and told him he was crazy about it. It transpired that Rodgers had picked up *Tales of the South Pacific* and loved it as well, but had forgotten who had recommended it to him. According to Logan:

> Dick said: I wrote down the name of the book, and was such a fool. I didn't jot down the name of Joshua Logan. . . . Had been going mad trying to think who told him about it, because he recalled that whoever told him had mentioned he owned the rights to the book.

PAGE 106: *Henry Fonda as the beloved Mister Roberts in the 1948 stage hit. Oscar Hammerstein's son, Billy, would serve as stage manager and consultant on the show, and Fonda would eventually marry his stepsister, Susan Blanchard. (Fonda would also be one of South Pacific's investors.)*

ABOVE: *The first formal photograph of the South Pacific production and creative team; Rodgers, Logan, and Hammerstein are joined by their coproducer, Leland Hayward.*

OPPOSITE: *Decommissioned army major Jo Mielziner was America's hottest stage designer of the late 1940s; his adroit and evocative designs for South Pacific would be key to its success.*

When Logan recounted his conversation to Leland Hayward, his producing partner hit the roof. They would now have to conclude negotiations with James Michener and then negotiate with Rodgers and Hammerstein who had, by 1948, hardened their reputations as tough cookies. Hayward visited Michener and offered him $500 outright for the stage rights to "Fo' Dolla'." Michener did not know much about the business part of show business, but he had been a shrewd manager of Macmillan's textbook accounts. "After a few minutes reflection," wrote Michener, "I told Hayward, 'I would always want to take risks on anything I did. Never an outright sale. Only royalties.'" Hayward knew he had been outsmarted and said he would get back to him. In the meantime, Hayward negotiated their partnership with Rodgers and Hammerstein, who demanded 51 percent of the eventual musical property to Hayward and Logan's 49 percent, which meant they would hold the controlling interest. Hayward wanted to chuck it all and go with another team, but Logan stood firm: why not the best, and let the chips fall where they may, he argued. Hayward acquiesced. Rodgers and Hammerstein were also savvy enough to want to buy the rights to all of Michener's nineteen stories.

Rodgers and Hammerstein's lawyer, Howard Reinheimer, offered Michener a one-percent royalty of the gross for the theatrical rights to all the stories. Michener was told that the playwright Lynn Riggs had been given 1.5 percent for the rights to the play that had been adapted into *Oklahoma!*, but that was "a real play. It had structure." Michener could argue that *Tales of the South Pacific* had several merits, but even he could not make a case for its structure. He took the 1 percent "and never had any regrets."

After these negotiations were successfully concluded, *Mister Roberts* opened on February 18 to cheering audiences. The very next day, all of New York's nine daily papers were filled with rave reviews, but the *New York Times* had the scoop on one item of particular interest: "Show to Be Based on Michener Tale." It was announced that Rodgers, Hammerstein, Hayward, and Logan would be producing the show jointly, and that Rodgers would, of course, write the score, while Hammerstein would handle the book and lyrics. The creative team set to work, with a projected Broadway opening around Christmastime 1948.

Michener set to work as well, getting his new novel, *The Fires of Spring*, ready for publication. The early part of

1948 had been a busy and emotionally exhausting time for Michener. He had been courted by several important agents, only to be disappointed when the most prestigious of them declined to represent *The Fires of Spring*. Macmillan wanted to keep him on as an editor, but Michener wanted to spend more time writing, and even a part-time schedule was of no interest to him. Michener had also moved back to his hometown of Doylestown and Hammerstein was amused to discover, after spending several weeks trying to track Michener down, that the author lived on Harvey Avenue, only a five-minute walk away from Hammerstein's farm. (Already neighbors, they became fast friends and professional colleagues.) Mostly, Michener wanted his book published. He decided to bring the manuscript to the Random House publishing company personally. He had always liked Random House because they were the only firm at the time that was racially integrated. Michener was particularly fond of the African American receptionist at Random House—she was the same woman who had sung in the original cast of *Carmen Jones*.

While Random House was deliberating the fate of *The Fires of Spring*, the *South Pacific* project got a burst of publicity that even money could not buy. On the afternoon of April 27, while Michener was in the middle of an

ABOVE: Across a crowded page spread, Ezio Pinza, as Don Giovanni, gazes at his next leading lady. Pinza sang the leading role in Mozart's opera over 200 times.

editing conference in his Macmillan offices, someone burst through the door, saying, "Jim! You've done it! You've won the Pulitzer Prize!" Indeed, to the surprise of many in the literary world—not the least of whom was Michener himself—*Tales of the South Pacific* had won the 1948 Pulitzer Prize for fiction. It was unusual for the Pulitzer committee to give an award to a series of short stories—or to a book that was not set in America, for that matter—but apparently the freshness of the book's approach carried the day. Michener was quoted as saying, "No one could have been more surprised than I. . . . Nor could anyone have been more pleased, for if I held no great brief for the stories as art, I was indelibly convinced that they could never be challenged as a truthful and sometimes probing analysis of men lost in a strange world." Rodgers and Hammerstein were more succinct; they cabled Michener from Los Angeles: "CONGRATULATIONS AND SALUTES TO YOU AND HOORAY FOR OUR JUDGEMENT EXCLAMATION POINT" Henceforth, the qualifier "Pulitzer Prize Winning Novel" would always appear on Michener's official credit on all programs and publicity for the musical.

Meanwhile, Rodgers and Hammerstein went to California to see how Mary Martin was getting on in the national tour of *Annie Get Your Gun*. They had been discussing the adaptation possibilities of Michener's book for months and if they had not exactly been getting nowhere, they still had not refined their dramatic focus. Initially, Hammerstein had been intrigued about somehow putting all the stories on stage, in a kind of woolly musical revue called Operation Alligator, but, as he told *Theater Arts* magazine, "we'd have got an impossible, crazy-quilt kind of play." Actually, Hammerstein's first instincts were not far off the mark. There had been several successful musical "anthologies" of military life on Broadway: Moss Hart's tribute to the Air Corps, *Winged Victory*; Harold Rome's revue about civilian life, *Call Me Mister*; and, of course, Berlin's *This Is the Army*. Hammerstein even flirted with basing the musical around the raffish, quixotic Tony Fry, whom he considered "the most attractive character" in the *Tales*. But, at the end of the day, Rodgers and Hammerstein had to concede that the most musically attractive stories in *Tales* were also the most romantic ones: "Fo' Dolla'," Joe Cable's saga of obsessive love; and "Our Heroine," the relationship of Nellie Forbush and Emile De Becque.

By the time of the late spring sojourn to Los Angeles, Hammerstein had fashioned an outline that was largely built around "Fo' Dolla'"—although, unable to lose Tony Fry completely, he turned Fry, who had dallied with many a local lass in the *Tales*, into Liat's lover. Still, as Rodgers and Hammerstein kept discussing the structure of the show, they were unhappy. "We were worried that people would call it *Madame Butterfly* all over again, just because the girl had slanting eyes, and the boy was a naval officer. And I couldn't get that Frenchman, De Becque, out of my mind. How could we use him? He was mature; mature things happened to him, important things. We began to flirt with the idea of making the Frenchman the leading character." If De Becque had lodged himself in Hammerstein's mind, he was also about to drop into his lap.

Edwin Lester, a major musical theater impresario on the West Coast, had created a $25,000 problem by the name of Ezio Pinza. In 1948, Pinza, at the age of 58, had an uncontested reputation as the most romantic, most stage-worthy, most accomplished lyric bass in the opera world. Although he had trained as a professional cyclist growing up in his native Italy, he made his stage debut in 1919, and performed at New York's Metropolitan Opera seven years later. He became the darling of the Met, performing with the company at least 800 times in such challenging roles as Boris Godunov and Don Giovanni, a signature role of which he sang more than 200 performances. In the mid-1940s he had even made the crossover to popular culture, singing serious ballads on Bing Crosby's radio show. His good looks and magnetism would serve him well and, as he (or his ghost writer—his English was appalling) said in his autobiography, "I had become restless, having practically exhausted the repertoire available for my voice and sung in every major opera house and concert house in the world. . . I was looking for new fields to conquer."

Pinza toyed with a Hollywood contract and made a cameo appearance in the film *Carnegie Hall*. He also considered a dramatic stage career but, always accustomed to a certain lifestyle, accepted Edwin Lester's offer to star in a new musical on the West Coast to the tune of $2,000 a week for a minimum of 12 weeks. So, on May 14, Pinza gave his last performance with the Metropolitan Opera and signed with Lester. The problems began—and ended—with the fact that Lester's new musical, called *Mr. Ambassador*, had not even been written and never would be. He was

ABOVE: *Any role you can play, I can play better. Mary Martin as Annie Oakley in the National Tour of* Annie Get Your Gun. *The demands of the part lowered her voice by an octave.*

stuck with Pinza's $25,000 contract. Lester met with Rodgers and Hammerstein at the Bel Air Hotel and presented them with his problem.

His problem became their solution. Lester gingerly broached the subject with Pinza and his wife, who assiduously guided his career, and lent them a copy of *Tales of the South Pacific*. "Sell me right away!" cried Pinza after he read the stories. Rodgers had never heard Pinza sing in English, so when he got back to New York he bought a copy of the only record Pinza had made in his adopted language—a black spiritual called "Deep River"—and promptly started negotiations with the singer. In June, when Pinza came back east to do a live radio broadcast, Rodgers and Hammerstein were in the audience. The reaction was so great from the crowd that any apprehensions vanished. They closed on a contract with Pinza which, among other considerations typical for an opera singer, included a clause that he not be asked to sing more than fifteen minutes of material per performance. (Pinza was actually not the first opera star to cross over to the legitimate musical stage, but no one of his magnitude had worked with anyone of Rodgers and Hammerstein's reputation.)

Having concluded their financial agreements with Pinza, the team realized that, indeed, the story of Emile and Nellie had to take dramaturgical precedence in the show— and that meant they needed a strong Nellie. Hammerstein said, "As long as we've got Pinza, let's go whole hog. Let's get Mary Martin to play Nellie." For Rodgers, this idea made complete sense. "Casting Mary was dramatically sound and connected with the way we were approaching the characters," he told *Theatre Arts* magazine. "We wanted to cast Nellie Forbush, our heroine, with somebody *like* Nellie Forbush." Martin had hailed from Texas, right across the border from Arkansas, and if any stage star of the 1940s could embody the optimistic charm of a navy nurse who wants to "see the world and learn about other people," it was Martin. Convincing her to do it was another story.

Ironically, Martin was already in the employ of Rodgers and Hammerstein, in the road company of *Annie Get Your Gun*. They called her in Los Angeles and asked how she would like to match her voice against Pinza's. At this point, after delivering Ethel Merman's songs eight performances a week, her bell-like soprano had sunk an octave lower than usual. "Good Lord!" she exclaimed to Rodgers on the long-distance line, "what will you do with two bassos?" Martin and her husband/manager, Richard Halliday, were about to drive back to the East Coast at the end of the summer and agreed at least to hear what Rodgers, Hammerstein, and Logan had in mind. She also took the opportunity to hear her potential leading man in concert. After hearing Pinza give a recital in Brooklyn, she was "floored" by his glorious voice but was deeply concerned that he would sing her into the next county if they were placed onstage together. Rodgers assured her that he would write a score in which she would never have to sing in competition with Pinza.

Rodgers was true to his word. In order to get a commitment out of Martin, Rodgers invited her and Halliday over to his Connecticut house (they lived nearby) to hear what he and Hammerstein had come up with so far. At this point, Hammerstein had written only the first scene between Emile and Nellie and an outline for the rest of the show. Josh Logan came by to read the dialogue—"Josh really outdid himself when he read that scene," recalled Hammerstein—and Rodgers and Hammerstein played and sang "A Cockeyed Optimist," "Twin Soliloquies" (the duet that allowed Pinza and Martin to sing without competing with each other), and "Some Enchanted Evening." They had given Martin and Halliday their best shot and asked them to go home, think it over, and call them back within seventy-two hours. Martin and Halliday stayed up talking until three o'clock in the morning. The song that really stuck with them was "Some Enchanted Evening." Even though Martin knew it was not her song, she knew that any show with that ballad was bound to be a memorable one. And, trouper that she was, she knew that anything which made Pinza look good would make her look good, too. Martin picked up the phone and called Rodgers. "Do we have to wait seventy-two hours to say, 'Yes'?" she asked.

Rodgers and Hammerstein had pulled off a coup by getting a major opera star to appear in a musical opposite one of the great leading ladies of the musical theater. Pinza and Martin were also about to break the bank. Rodgers and Hammerstein's lawyer went to Pinza and explained the problem: Martin expected to be paid as much as he was. "Fine," he said. "This really is your problem, not mine." However, he recounted in his autobiography that "it did not take me long to realize that the problem was mine as well." Both Pinza and Martin accepted the fact that the whole of the show would be even greater with their two halves and each

ABOVE: In this rare photo, Richard Rodgers shows his affection, and trust, in his new leading lady.

could move him until the heavy machinery was lifted off the mangled man.

"Come on," the MP's would shout. "Get away from there! Break it up!"

And the stolid fellow would reply, "He was ma' bes' buddy." Then everyone left him alone.

I doubt if Lt. Cable ever thought about himself in just those terms, but he knew very well that he mustn't brood too long over that tousle-headed girl in Germantown. He knew—even though his tour of battle duty on Guadalcanal had been short—that consuming passions are better kept in check. They burn out too damned quick, otherwise.

And yet there was the need for some kind of continuing interest in something. He'd had a pup, but the damned thing had grown up, as pups will, and it was off somewhere on another island. He'd done a lot of reading, too. Serious stuff, about mechanics, and a little history, too. But after a while reading becomes a bore.

Bloody Mary of course was different. She was old and repulsive, with her parched skin and her jagged teeth. But finer than any dog or any book, she was a sentient being with a mind, a personality, a history, a human memory, and—Lt. Cable winced at the idea—a soul. Unlike the restless tropical sea, she grew tired and slept. Unlike the impenetrable jungle, she could be perceived. Unlike the papayas and the road vines, she lived a generation, grew old, and died. She was subject to human laws, to a human rate of living, to a human world. And by heavens, she was an interesting old woman.

"She has a husband," Lt. Cable wrote his sweetheart. "She says he is on another island where the French have moved all the young girls. She lives here to trade with the Americans. I think if the French knew this they would deport her to the other island, too. But since she stays here and behaves herself, I have no mind to report her. In fact, I find talking French and Pidgin English with her amusing and instructive. I may even arrange to take a few days off and visit the other island with her when she takes money to her husband. She says he will be surprised, for she has not less than nine hundred dollars. That will be a great deal of money in Tonkin. In fact, it would be a lot of money right in Philadelphia."

It was about two weeks after this letter that Atabrine Benny arranged a boat trip to the island upon which Bloody Mary's husband lived. Benny had to see to it that all Tonks had their supply of atabrine, and he visited the outlying islands monthly. This time he agreed to take Bloody Mary along, and at the last minute Lt. Cable decided to

146

join them. He brought with him a mosquito net, a revolver, a large thermos jug of water, a basket of tinned food, and a bottle of atabrine tablets.

"My God, lieutenant," Benny said. "I got a million of 'em."

Everyone laughed, and the boat shoved off. I was down in the pre-dawn dark to bid Benny farewell and instruct him to pick me up a wild boar's tusk, if he could. That was when I first met Lt. Cable. He was a tall fellow, about six feet one. He was lean and weighed not more than one hundred and seventy-five pounds. He had not the graceful motions of a natural athlete, but he was a powerfully competent man. I thought then that he would probably give a good account of himself in a fight. He had a shock of unruly blond hair. His face, although not handsome, was masculine; and he carried himself as if he were one of the young men to whom the world will one day belong. To this quiet assurance he added a little of the Marine's inevitable cockiness. He was an attractive fellow, and it was clearly to be seen that Bloody Mary, the embattled Tonk, shared my opinion. Ignoring Atabrine Benny completely, she sat in the bows with Cable and talked French in barbarous accents.

The island to which Benny was going lay sixteen miles to the east. It was a large and brooding island, miasmic with malaria, old fetishes, sickness and deep shadows. It was called Vanicoro, and in the old times was known as a magic place. Four peaks lined the center of the island. Two of them were active volcanoes. Only the bravest natives dared live on Vanicoro, and they were the last to give up cannibalism.

As the small boat drew near the island Bloody Mary pointed at Vanicoro and assured Cable, "You like! You like very much!" The Marine studied the volcanoes. Upon them the red glow of sunrise rapidly lightened into the gold of early morning. Mists rose from them like smoke from writhing lava.

"That's right pretty," Benny called back. "Look at them hills smoke!"

Lt. Cable watched the mists of Vanicoro surrendering to the early sun. And then, as a child, while playing with an old familiar toy, sees a new thing from the corner of his eye, Cable suddenly saw, without looking at it, the island of Bali-ha'i.

"Benny!" he cried. "There's another island!"

There was another island! Bali-ha'i was an island of the sea, a jewel of the vast ocean. It was small. Like a jewel, it could be perceived in one loving glance. It was neat. It had majestic cliffs facing the open sea. It had a jagged hill to give it character. It was green like something ever youthful, and it seemed to curve itself like a woman into

147

ABOVE: Oscar Hammerstein's personal copy of Tales of the South Pacific. This page is open to the "Fo' Dolla'" chapter. His notes, scrawled in the margins reveal, left, his impulse to integrate the story of Lt. Cable with that of Nellie Forbush. The right-hand page displays his excitement over using Bali Ha'i for a song.

agreed to take a smaller (but equal) paycheck of $2000 per week in order to appear opposite each other. Pinza agreed to Martin having first billing—"I reacted with something like, 'Ladies first,' and that was that"—but insisted that there be no "and" between their names, which might have implied that she outranked him. With egos in check, and the check in the bank, the crucial casting of the show was solved.

Down on the Doylestown farm, things had not progressed much with the script adaptation since the "audition" for Mary Martin. Hammerstein had, indeed, written the compelling first scene, which defied musical theater convention by bringing the two stars on stage about three minutes after the curtain went up. He knew that *South Pacific* would have a tremendous amount of dramatic material, and there was no time to waste; start with the leading characters' stories and hook the audience that way—their story was compelling enough on its own merits. Hammerstein had created an outline that placed Emile and Nellie's story against the subplot of Lieutenant Cable's romance with Liat—by now, there was no doubt that the "Fo' Dolla" characters were going to be secondary to the more mature love story. Hammerstein still had a problem with how to intertwine the stories and he solved it with amazing ingenuity.

Through the years, the common assumption is that *South Pacific* was based on only two of Michener's stories, a misconception somewhat abetted by Hammerstein's own assertion to this effect. (It also did not help that "Our Heroine"—the Emile and Nellie story—was left out of the first paperback edition of *Tales of the South Pacific* for misguided reasons of space, leading many critics and viewers to believe that this plot was purely an invention of Rodgers and Hammerstein's.) Actually, there is hardly a tale in Michener's book that does not get raided in one form or another: A throwaway line about the heat on the tin roof of a Quonset hut from "The Coral Sea" adds to the tension of an Act Two scene; the Professor, a minor character from "The Airstrip at Konora," becomes Luther Billis' sidekick; the names of Emile's children in the musical—Ngana and Jerome—are taken from two of the Remittance Man's comrades in "The Cave." In fact, it is from "The Cave" that Hammerstein borrowed his critical plot point. Hammerstein decided to recast "the Remittance Man"—the brave British individual who goes behind enemy lines to transmit Japanese troop movements to the Allies"—as Emile de Becque (the "de" of his name now set in lowercase). The secret mission gives de Becque a way to redeem Nellie's rejection of him, and also brings de Becque together with Cable—who initiates the mission, another Hammerstein invention—for the crucial climax of the show. The heroics of the mission (and the passion behind it) transforms Emile de Becque from his role in Michener's story as a kind of Rick Blaine (Humphrey Bogart's cynical character in *Casablanca*) into a Victor Laszlo, a partisan patriot.

As impressive as the outline was—and it was very impressive—it simply was not being fleshed out fast enough for Rodgers and Hayward, who had to contemplate rescheduling the Christmas opening. The musical end of things was moving easily for Rodgers—it usually did—especially after Michener told him that the stereotypical sounds of the South Pacific such as a steel guitar or a marimba did not actually exist there at all. As Rodgers wrote in the *New York Herald-Tribune*:

To my amazement and joy I found out that in this particular area of the Pacific there was no instrumental music of any kind and that the nearest approach to it was simple percussion. . . .I realized I could use what is known as a legitimate orchestra, with no trick instruments of any kind for atmosphere. I would also be allowed to do what I had always wanted to do by way of construction—give each character the sort of music that went with the particular character, rather than the locale in which we found him.

Still, in his collaboration with Hammerstein, he nearly always wrote the music after Hammerstein submitted the lyrics—and Rodgers had been waiting around for more of them. When they were not forthcoming, he called Logan in to turn up the heat.

"Josh, I know absolutely nothing about army behavior or how a sergeant talks to a general and vice versa," admitted Hammerstein to Logan when he called him on the phone. Hammerstein had never been in the military, never been comfortable with its authority, and was completely stumped as to how to write a show with so much serious military material. (He also admitted he did not know how to write a girl from Little Rock, Arkansas—she kept sounding to him like a Times Square showgirl.) Logan volunteered to give Hammerstein what help he could; after all, he was from the South and had spent four years in the Army. Hammerstein gratefully accepted the assistance, so Logan went to Bucks County with his wife, armed with a recording device called a Dictaphone and a secretary. He planned to stay just for the weekend.

Logan wound up staying nearly two weeks, during which time, as he told an interviewer:

In the mornings Hammerstein would write alone, and in the afternoons and nights until two in the morning, we worked together. I was dictating all the scenes that had to do with the military—Cable, Harbison, and Brackett. We switched the Dictaphone back and forth, he would talk Emile and I would talk Nellie. At two or three in the morning, we'd wake our wives and they'd listen to the scenes.

Hammerstein and Logan worked together in a welter of depression and elation, acting scenes out and bouncing the material back and forth. At one point, they found themselves hopelessly stuck at the end of Act One.

ABOVE: Logan and Hammerstein. Hammerstein rarely worked with a co-librettist, yet their collaboration yielded a Pulitzer Prize-winning script, even though the contractual agreements were strained.

OPPOSITE: The finish line. After six years of parallel lives; at war and at peace; in New York, in Europe, in the South Pacific and back again, Logan, Rodgers, Hammerstein, and Michener join together with Mary Martin to celebrate the beginning of their extraordinary collaboration, 1948.

Nellie had returned to Emile's plantation and there was a huge dinner party scene with guests and dancing natives and it seemed as if they would never get to the important part—Emile getting Nellie to accept him again. "Suppose we start *after* the party?" one of them said to the other. "And we dictated that scene in six minutes and it has never changed except for one line," recounted Logan. At one point, Logan got so excited by the work that he shouted, "If this isn't the damnedest show that's ever been written, I'll eat my hat." Hammerstein topped him: "It'll be Goddamnedest of all the most Goddamn shows produced since Cain and Abel started charades!"

When Logan returned to New York to allow Hammerstein to polish the script and start writing his lyrics, he was in high spirits. Rodgers liked what he had read, and so had Michener who, other than to jot down some ideas for Hammerstein about what kind of schemes an enterprising Seabee such as Luther Billis might be up to in his spare time, had practically no input on the musical. Michener was thrilled with the progress, thoroughly enjoying those precious moments when Rodgers and Hammerstein might play through a rough draft of their latest song. (He later recalled that Rodgers and Hammerstein "were inwardly burning because of the reception accorded *Allegro*.") "I cannot imagine a writer who could be more satisfied with a stage translation than I am with *South Pacific*," he wrote in the *New York Times*. "I can only say that they have accomplished a remarkable feat of juggling without ever mussing an eyebrow of one of the characters."

Logan was certain he was about to direct the most important production of his career, but he was beside himself with anxiety because he had also written half of it and was convinced that no one would ever know it. (He had a right to be proud of his achievements as a writer—that March, he and Thomas Heggen would win the Tony Award for Best Play for *Mister Roberts*, beating out *A Streetcar Named Desire*.) Logan's wife had convinced him to speak to Hammerstein about sharing author credit of the book to *South Pacific*. Logan timorously approached Hammerstein, who told him, "I wish I'd said it first. I'm sorry you had to. Of course you must have credit. You wrote it as much as I did." Logan was immensely relieved, but the next day Hammerstein called on Logan to inform him of the finality of the business arrangement he had discussed with Rodgers and their lawyer: Logan would get credit with Hammerstein as coauthor of

the book, but the size of their billing would be 60% of Rodgers and Hammerstein's billing for music and lyrics. What was more, Logan would not share in the copyright and would not participate in any of the author's royalties.

This sudden reversal shocked and pained Logan—he even felt sorry for Hammerstein, who, in Logan's opinion, was simply toeing the line that Rodgers and the firm's legal representation had drawn. Still, Logan believed so much in the project that he accepted the terms, although the inequity would gnaw at him for the rest of his life. Leland Hayward had little sympathy; he was fighting his own battles with Rodgers and Hammerstein when they threatened to dissolve their producing partnership after Hayward made noises about producing a Sidney Kingsley play *Detective Story*, which might arrive on Broadway before *South Pacific* (Hayward sold his interest to Lindsay and Crouse and it opened two weeks before *South Pacific*). Hayward had no trouble getting the fifty investors together to pony up the $225,000 required to open the show (they included Billy Wilder, Thomas Heggen,

and Mary Martin). In a gesture of generosity far from the way they treated Logan, Rodgers and Hammerstein offered Michener one share of the show, at the cost of $4,500. When Michener demurred, saying he did not have that kind of money, Rodgers and Hammerstein said they would front him the money. He could have the $4,500 taken out of his share of the profits as they rolled it; *South Pacific* was going to be a sure thing and they wanted to cut Michener in on it. That one share would eventually allow Michener to quit his job and devote himself to being a full-time fiction writer.

As 1948 drew to an exhausted close, the show had finally come together—the cast was nearly set, the script and score was finished, the contracts were drawn up—and it was time to rest up for the rehearsals which would begin in February of the coming year. One last thing: the title of Michener's book had been officially shortened (as they almost always are in musical adaptations) to *South Pacific* because, as Rodgers said, "People were making dirty puns on the word 'Tales' and it was beginning to get tiresome."

YOUNGER THAN SPRINGTIME

I touch your hand,
And my arms grow strong,
Like a pair of birds
That burst with song.
My eyes look down
At your lovely face,
And I hold the world
In my embrace.

Younger than springtime are you,
Softer than starlight are you;
Warmer than winds of June are the gentle lips you gave me.
Gayer than laughter are you,
Sweeter than music are you;
Angel and lover, heaven and earth,
Are you to me.

And when your youth and joy invade my arms
And fill my heart, as now they do,
Then, younger than springtime am I,
Gayer than laughter am I,
Angel and lover, heaven and earth,
Am I with you.

JOSH LOGAN HAD TO FIGHT WITH HIS COLLABORATORS
TO HAVE CABLE APPEAR BARE-CHESTED ON STAGE
WHEN THE LIGHTS CAME UP AFTER HE HAD MADE
LOVE TO LIAT.

Lieutenant Cable's rhapsody of newfound romance to the Tonkinese girl, Liat, took a long time in arriving. Granted, it was a difficult song to write; in Michener's tale, Cable expresses his ardor physically—he deflowers Liat within minutes of meeting her, with only her white cotton shirt separating them from the dirt floor of her hut. The conventions of 1949 would not have permitted such an erotically charged moment in a Broadway musical. (Josh Logan had to fight with his collaborators to have Cable appear bare-chested on stage when the lights came up after he had made love to Liat.)

Still, conventions do not quite excuse the anemic first pass at the song by Hammerstein, who, if Logan can be credited, wrote the following for Liat to sing as Cable gets off the boat at Bali Ha'i:

> My friend, my friend,
> Is coming around the bend.

The next attempt was a step in the right direction— it was sung by Cable and at least expressed some degree of passion:

> Suddenly lovely,
> Suddenly my life is lovely.
> Suddenly living
> Certainly looks good to me.
> Suddenly happy,
> Suddenly my heart is happy,
> Is it a girl?
> Could be, could be!

Still, for Logan, the sentiment was too "lightweight" for a "hot, lusty boy" who was about to be consumed by a sexual obsession, and the tune, while quite jaunty, seemed inappropriate as well.

Rodgers and Hammerstein were not pleased, but came back a third time with new lyrics to a melody called "My Wife" which was cut from *Allegro*. The new song seemed to fit the bill beautifully and "Younger Than Springtime" became the fourth song of the show to join the Hit Parade. The footnote to posterity is the melody for "Suddenly Lovely" was reused for Rodgers and Hammerstein's next show, *The King and I*, where with new lyrics, it was called "Getting to Know You." You can still sing these lyrics to that tune.

PAGE 119: *William Tabbert and Betta St. John, original cast. His arms grow very strong; director Josh Logan thought that male nudity—from the waist up—was very provocative and he used the effect in many productions.*

OPPOSITE: *Post-coital reverie: Edward Baker-Duly and Elaine Tan in Trevor Nunn's 2001 production*

ABOVE: *John Kerr and France Nuyen embrace in the film version.*

CHAPTER EIGHT
1949

"The New York opening may be a musical's most exciting moment, but close to it is the first reading of the full score and book," wrote Josh Logan in his memoirs. "Will it or won't it?"

The artists assembled on the bare stage of the Majestic Theatre on the morning of February 7 had done everything in their power to make sure that *South Pacific* "will." Rodgers and Hammerstein had chosen difficult material to adapt but, as was their wont, they made no concessions to convention—they let the story itself point the way to go. "There will be little native stuff," Rodgers told the *Los Angeles Times* shortly before rehearsals began. "There is no grass skirt business, no steel guitar or other such Hawaiian nonsense on these islands. There will be no stage numbers or line dancing, no chorus girl lines. The singers move about the stage in normal movement as if they are acting out a straight book story. Both the music and the dances will be a definitive part of the book story." Rodgers and Hammerstein also needed this show to be a hit, as Ted Chapin, president of the Rodgers and Hammerstein Organization points out in his introduction, because *Allegro* had so disappointed audiences and themselves.

In conjunction with Logan, Rodgers and Hammerstein had assembled the forty-one-person cast, hiring the last actor only five days before rehearsals began. Luther Billis was played by the bulbous Myron McCormick, a Princeton chum of Logan's, who was an old Broadway hand at playing ornery everymen. Juanita Hall, an African American veteran of many musicals and plays, portrayed Bloody Mary. William Tabbert, an up-and-coming young actor, was given the role of Cable, once he had followed orders by Logan to physically shape up for the part; his paramour in the show, Liat, was played by Betta St. John, making her first and only Broadway appearance.

PAGE 122: *What it was like to be in* South Pacific: *this shot, taken from the rear of the Shubert Theater, Boston, looking out to the audience, captures a rehearsal of the Thanksgiving Follies. Martin Wolfson as Captain Brackett can be seen at center.*

ABOVE: Logan, who served as the show's choreographer—we'd call it "musical staging" today—demonstrates a step.

The rank and file of officers, enlisted men, nurses, and villagers were filled out by a wide range of performers with a wide range of experience. Several of the actors playing servicemen had themselves served in the war only a few years previously; Don Fellows, playing the part of Lt. Buzz Adams (somewhere along the way "Bus Adams" became "Buzz") had even served briefly as a marine on the island of Espiritu Santo in 1943.

On the design front, it was a foregone conclusion that Jo Mielziner would do the sets and lights—not only did his stepbrother, Kenneth MacKenna start the whole thing, but they were both investors in the show. Mielziner was on an unprecedented roll—in addition to *Carousel* and *Allegro*, he had designed *Mister Roberts*, *Streetcar*, and *Death of a Salesman*, which was about to open three days after *South Pacific*'s first rehearsal. Mielziner had also been a major in the United States Army during the war, running a unit that designed camouflage for troops overseas. Costumes were provided by Motley, a joint pseudonym for a group of English designers; the chores were actually handled by only one of the designers, Elizabeth Montgomery. Three of Rodgers' most trusted musical colleagues were on board as well: Robert Russell Bennett to handle orchestrations, Salvatore Dell'Isola to serve as musical director, and Trude Rittmann, who would not only compose the dance arrangements but also sit by Logan's side during rehearsal, in case he had a moment of musical inspiration for atmospheric underscoring.

Logan rehearsed this musical differently from any other show on which he had worked; in fact, he rehearsed differently than any other director even had on a musical. Logan took pride in his Stanislavsky training; he carefully created a mood on stage and made sure that every actor had a definitive character, a motivation, and an integral part in the larger dramatic and stage picture. Rodgers praised his ability "to follow a rare, subdued technique . . . his extraordinary sense of balance has made it possible for the small values in the songs to create a large effect." Logan was fascinated with underscoring and used it to greater emotional effect in *South Pacific* than had ever been heard in a musical; he asked Rittmann to extend the ascending chords in "Twin Soliloquies" to express Nellie and Emile's romantic intensity while they raise their cognac snifters and gaze into each other's eyes; the effect was more powerful than any words or lyrics. Similarly, he had her create a tense underscoring for Cable's personal anxiety in Act Two. (Rittmann created these musical moments, and more, with the full trust and support of Rodgers, whose music was always the basis for the underscoring.)

As director, Logan extended his specificity to the actors. There would be no generalized group of chorus boys and pretty girls; each member of the cast would have a name and, in most cases, a rank (but no serial number). One nurse was named "Ensign Sue Yaeger" after an old school chum of Mary Martin's; another was named "Ensign Lisa Minelli" (that's "Lisa" with a "S"). The non-com Seabees and sailors were each given $50 and instructed to go to one of the Army/Navy surplus stores along West 42nd Street and buy whatever they thought their characters would wear. Don Fellows relied on his own wartime experience and outfitted Buzz Adams with a non-regulation baseball cap worn at a jaunty angle and thick black ankle boots. Other cast members customized their gear according to their characters and their whims. It was exactly the kind of variegated reality that Logan wanted.

The realistic style of *South Pacific* extended to its choreography: there was none. Each of Rodgers and Hammerstein's previous shows had featured the choreography of Agnes de Mille, and hers was ground-breaking choreography that elevated the show and changed the face of the American musical. Here, they did without because that was what the show demanded. Logan was in charge of "musical staging," which usually amounted to him encouraging his actors to behave in character, informally, and in time with the music. "The thing was rehearsed very much the way a dramatic show is," recalled Rodgers. Unlike a typical musical, the cast was not broken into its component parts during rehearsal. "There was nothing for [the navy nurses and the Seabees] to rehearse that didn't involve the principals. So everything had to be done in one building."

The four weeks of New York rehearsals went smoothly. There were no ego clashes, no car wrecks (although Don Fellows noticed that when Rodgers did not like something Logan had staged he would call the director to the rear of the house for "a word" and it would be quickly changed). Mary Martin recalled that the "gypsy run-through"—the informal run of the show presented to friends and professional colleagues in a bare theater before the technical elements are added—was met with one of the

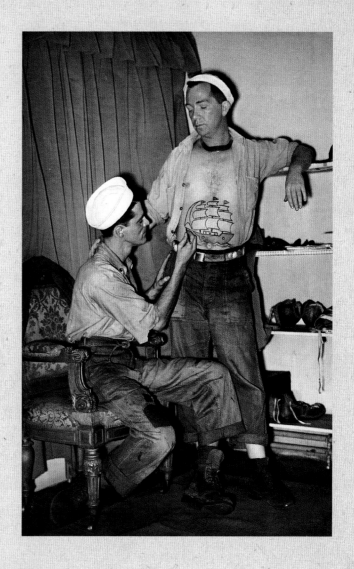

ABOVE: Not official uniform; Luther Billis needs his tattoo for the show. This is Glen Fontane and Ray Walston backstage in the London production.

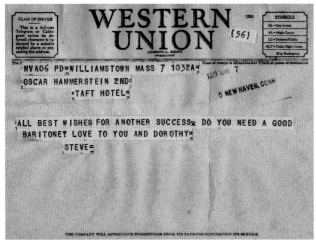

ABOVE, TOP: A rare program from the show's debut out of town, March 1949.

ABOVE, BOTTOM: A congratulatory telegram sent from Williams College, Massachusetts, to Oscar Hammerstein. It comes from Hammerstein's young protégé and friend, Stephen Sondheim.

OPPOSITE, TOP: Cut from out-of-town: William Tabbert sings "My Girl Back Home" to Mary Martin

OPPOSITE, BOTTOM LEFT: Juanita Hall as Bloody Mary, in keen anticipation.

OPPOSITE, BOTTOM RIGHT: Hammerstein's typewritten lyrics

most genuinely enthusiastic reactions of her entire career. It would now take a week of tryout performances at the Shubert Theatre in New Haven and then two weeks at the Shubert in Boston to iron out whatever problems existed; there were not many.

There were, out of necessity and time concerns, some changes in the songs and in the song order. During rehearsals, the song that would become "Younger Than Springtime" would be summarily overhauled, but with the exception of a song called "Now is the Time," in which Emile works up the courage to ask Nellie back, the Act One order of songs in New Haven was exactly what it would be when the show opened in New York. Act Two contained a duet for Emile and Nellie called "Will My Love Come Back to Me," which stayed in as long as Boston, but it never really registered, so it too was cut. Cable also had a song which made it through Boston called "My Girl Back Home," a nicely melodic "puzzlement" over his culture shock:

> How far away!
> Philadelphia, P.A.
> Princeton, N.J.—
> How far are they
> From coconut palms
> And banyan trees
> And coral sands
> And Tonkinese!

"My Girl Back Home" was simply overwhelmed by the culmination of dramatic events in Act Two and was cut prior to New York; it reappeared in the subsequent film and television versions, sung as a duet between Cable and Nellie.

As the scenery was shipped off to New Haven to await the arrival of the cast, the only person truly unhappy was Ezio Pinza. He had been doing beautifully with the songs (all fifteen minutes of them) and he and Martin had a mutual lovefest, with a nary a note of conflict between them. Pinza was simply used to the opera world where, once a performer mastered a role, it never changed. Rehearsals for a new Broadway musical are all about change. "In *South Pacific*," he wrote in his autobiography, "one never was sure. . . . The words never stood still. One was no longer sure of anything except that the notes and the words would be reshuffled once more the next day." Pinza was convinced

MY GIRL BACK HOME

My girl back home -
I'd almost forget!
A blue-eyed kid -
I liked her a lot.
We got engaged -
Both families glad;
And I was told
 By my uncle and Dad
That if I were clever and able
They'd make me a part of a partnership -
Cable, Cable, - and Cable!

How far away!
Philadelphia, P. A.
Princeton, N. J. -
How far are they
From coconut palms
And banyan trees
And coral sands
And Tonkinese!

ABOVE: South Pacific was auditioning for its ensemble through the dead of winter, January 1949. Here, potential Navy nurses in the South Pacific bundle up. Jack Prenner is at the piano.

OPPOSITE: Logan demands a certain oomph from Mary Martin's treatment of Barbara Luna and Michael de Leon, as Ngana and Jerome; being the good sport she is, she complies.

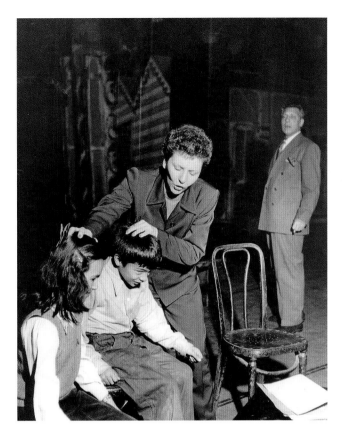

Logan wanted him out of the show (Logan did not—he just found Pinza's accent impenetrable and, for the moment, preferred to leave Pinza to his own devices) and told his wife on the drive up to New Haven that it would be best for all concerned if he volunteered to leave and return to the Met, where the audience already loved him. "If it's the audience you're worried about," his wife told him, "why not let the audience decide for itself?"

On the evening of March 7, they did. Pinza was a smash from the moment he opened his mouth to sing. Mary Martin captivated everyone. It was an enchanted evening for everyone except Logan, whose emotions and anxiety got the better of him; he thought it was a flop because Martin failed to get the "money" applause in two of her numbers. The next day's *New Haven Register* proclaimed that "*South Pacific* should make history. . . the magic of *Oklahoma!* and *Carousel* is magnified." The Boston audiences reacted much the same way a week later. Elliot Norton of the *Boston Post* announced that "with Joshua Logan to stage it brilliantly . . . Richard Rodgers and Oscar Hammerstein 2nd have created another great musical show. It is impossible in a small space to do more than hint at the wonders of *South Pacific*." *The Boston Herald* concluded: "South *Terrific*—and then some!" One Boston critic simply did not bother to file his weekend

review because he said the show was "just about perfect." This actually made Rodgers and Hammerstein sore: "He might at least have made some suggestions."

From the creators' point of view however, the show was still running long (as producers, they would have to pay the stagehands overtime), so some discreet cuts were made with the help of Emlyn Williams, a British playwright and friend of Logan's. They mostly affected some of Billis' business in Act One and the preparation for "Operation Alligator" in Act Two. Some of Nellie's prejudicial reaction to Emile's children was toned down and several unnecessary references to the South Pacific scrupulously drafted in from Michener's book were excised. The show was in fighting trim for its opening night at the Majestic Theatre on April 7.

Hayward and his colleagues were able to do something miraculous—they were able to return some money to their investors on the evening of the first preview. Originally budgeted at $225,000, *South Pacific* actually cost $165,000 to open on Broadway because the out-of-town try-outs had gone so well that the money set aside to provide new sets, costumes, or orchestrations were not needed. An advance sale of $500,000, the largest in Broadway history up to that time, was still growing. The opening night was one of the most eagerly anticipated in several seasons and a huge party had been planned on the roof at the St. Regis Hotel. The list of first-nighters read like the Theater Hall of Fame: Irving Berlin, George Abbott, Elia Kazan, Rex Harrison, David O. Selznick, Katharine Hepburn, Agnes de Mille, John O'Hara, Henry Fonda, George S. Kaufman, Moss and Kitty Carlisle Hart, Jack Benny, Howard Lindsay, Russel Crouse, Yip Harburg as well as a friend of Hammerstein's from Bucks County, "Foxie" Sondheim. Her son, Steve, came down from college in Williamstown, and, according to theatrical legend, was introduced to the twenty-one-year-old guest of Richard Rodgers' daughter, Mary, in the aisle during intermission. His name was Harold Prince.

James Michener was there, too, of course, with his new wife. Apart from hearing a few songs early on and submitting some thoughts about Luther Billis, he happily stayed away from the fray, seeing the show for the first time at its dress rehearsal in New Haven. He did not mind at all: "I have never resented a penny paid to others for the work they did on my stories, for they knew the secrets required for transmuting words into images and I did not. In *South Pacific* the conversion was miraculous." Michener loved Hammerstein and Logan's original creation, Captain Brackett, as the catchall character for navy authority, and was "bitterly envious" that he had not thought of having Luther Billis—rather than Buzz Adams—cause a $600,000 rescue mission at sea. He did have one cavil, however— he did not like the fact that de Becque's four daughters were substituted with a boy and a girl: "Somehow—and this may be a crazy idea—I think the character of de Becque stands more clearly defined when surrounded by daughters."

Even that reservation would have stood out in relief to the raves delivered by the press the next morning. Brooks Atkinson, back on the job for the *New York Times*, wrote that the show was "magnificent . . . you will find high standards of characterization and acting throughout . . . as lively, warm, fresh and beautiful as we all hoped it would be." The *Journal-American* said, "The American theater has a reputation for the worthiness of its musicals. *South Pacific* will, in the long run, enhance it. It has already!" *Variety* commented that "Rodgers and Hammerstein have not only done it again—they've topped themselves." Martin was praised for the performance of her career and Pinza became an immediate matinee idol and Broadway superstar. *South Pacific* had become the smash that its creators had dreamed it would be.

The opening night was an evening to remember for even the most jaded of theatergoers, but for Harold Prince, just beginning his career in George Abbott's office, it "was and remains the most romantic musical I have ever seen," as he recounted on the occasion of the fiftieth anniversary of the show's opening. It also represented a technical leap forward on the musical theater stage, which had a profound effect on Prince:

> On that night, there were two travelers [show curtains], one going each direction, all the way across the stage. It was possible to continue the story in front of one, between two, and upstage of the second one, so you had three levels of activity, very much what in film you'd call "dissolves." Josh Logan did that, and the show just continued seamlessly from beginning to end.

ABOVE: *From Sir with Love: the recently knighted Sir Laurence Olivier greets Martin and Pinza backstage.*

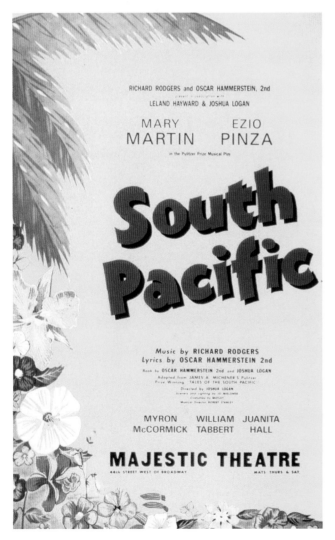

A week after the opening, Rodgers sent a gracious letter of thanks to Michener:

Any time I was faced with a very real crisis of having to have you hear the material, I found you so receptive, enthusiastic, and understanding, that the next time it came a little easier until eventually it became clear that Michener was going to like it. I can't tell you what this meant to me but we have all participated in a tremendous success and an event that will surely make theatrical history. It is something for all of us to be proud of and you, as the originator of the whole deal, should and must be the proudest. I know that I am of you.

Michener was proud, too; the success of the musical version of his stories would do more to elevate his profile and provide a solid basis for his continued career as a novelist than the Pulitzer Prize did. He took his new celebrity in characteristic stride, however; at a literary luncheon in his honor, he paraphrased Lord Byron's comment after the successful publication of his *Childe Harold's Pilgrimage* in 1812: "I went to bed an unknown and woke to find Ezio Pinza famous."

LEFT: A Broadway hit: program and poster from the original production.

OPPOSITE: Long before there were Phantom of the Opera *coffee mugs and* Mary Poppins *umbrellas,* South Pacific *led the way in Broadway product endorsements. These elegant scarves were joined by* South Pacific *lipsticks, ties, and perfumes.*

1949

Mary Martin...scintillating star of "South Pacific"

"Some Enchanted Evening"

...*go "South Pacific" with Mary Martin!*

wear COHAMA'S* exclusive pure silk squares

Cohama knows the score...of "South Pacific"...transposes smash hit tunes into exotically colorful designs†...60 exciting color combinations...36 inch squares of pure silk, ready for hemming. Go and see them...buy them for yourself and for gifts! 13 patterns in all, each in a variety of colors. "Some Enchanted Evening" • "Honey Bun" • "I'm Gonna Wash That Man.." • "Bali Ha'i" • "A Cock-eyed Optimist" • "Bloody Mary" • "Curtain Call" • "Happy Talk" • "There Is Nothin' Like a Dame" • "Dites-Moi" • "Younger Than Springtime" • "Thanksgiving Show" • "A Wonderful Guy"

(in reduced sizes)

"Younger than Springtime"

"Bali Ha'i"

"A Wonderful Guy"

"Honey Bun"

Priced so low you'll want to buy them all. In the Fabric Department only — of these and many other fine stores throughout the country:

MACY'S, NEW YORK   MARSHALL FIELD, CHICAGO   J. L. HUDSON, DETROIT   KAUFMANN'S, PITTSBURGH   JORDAN MARSH, BOSTON

COHAMA *fabrics*
A division of United Merchants and Manufacturers, Inc.

*Reg. U. S. Pat. Of.   †By exclusive arrangement with the owners of "South Pacific"

MAGAZINE, OCTOBER 30, 1949.   3

★ 133 ★

HAPPY TALK

Happy talk,
Keep talkin' happy talk,
Talk about things you'd like to do.
You gotta have a dream;
If you don't have a dream,
How you gonna have a dream come true?

    Talk about a moon
    Floatin' in de sky,
    Lookin' like a lily on a lake;
    Talk about a bird
    Learnin' how to fly,
    Makin' all de music he can make——

Happy talk,
Keep talkin' happy talk,
Talk about things you'd like to do.
You gotta have a dream;
If you don't have a dream,
How you gonna have a dream come true?

    Talk about a star
    Lookin' like a toy,
    Peakin' t'rough de branches of a tree;
    Talk about a girl,
    Talk about a boy,
    Countin' all de ripples on de sea——

Happy talk,
Keep talkin' happy talk,
Talk about things you'd like to do.
You gotta have a dream;
If you don't have a dream,
How you gonna have a dream come true?

    Talk about a boy
    Sayin' to a girl:
    "Golly, baby! I'm a lucky cuss!"
    Talk about de girl
    Sayin' to de boy:
    "You an'me is lucky to be us!"

Happy talk,
Keep talkin' happy talk,
Talk about things you'd like to do.
You gotta have a dream;
If you don't have a dream,
How you gonna have a dream come true?
    If you don't talk happy
    An' you never have a dream,
    Den you'll never have a dream come true.

One week after *South Pacific* opened, Joshua Logan wrote a piece in the *New York Times* about his directorial choices for the show:

The number that most people ask about is "Happy Talk" in which Betta St. John does the little finger dance, illustrating her mother's song. This was one of the last songs that Dick and Oscar wrote in the show. [They initially resisted, thinking that there was no way Logan could stage the number.] I took Juanita Hall and Betta St. John and William Tabbert down to the lobby of the theater, where we had another piano, and Juanita started singing it for me. I had had some idea in the back of my mind that Liat could be telling Joe Cable what a beautiful, lotus-eating life they could live by illustrating what her mother was singing. We had had so few opportunities in the show to indicate what kind of character Liat was that Dick suggested this might be a chance to use Betta's ability to dance.

Actually, Juanita Hall started to sing and I asked Betta to place Joe Cable into a sitting position, facing her. As the words "happy talk" were sung I imagined the two of them speaking in the same rhythm of the song. This suggested the little gesture with the fingers as two mouths talking. Gestures occurred to me and her at the same time. Within ten minutes, perhaps even less than that, the entire number was finished. Betta worked out the little dance from the gestures in the song. The next day the mother joined her in the gestures during the last chorus.

In his collected *Lyrics*, Oscar Hammerstein wrote, "The word 'dream' is a much overworked word. . . . When I started to write my most recent set of lyrics for *South Pacific*, I made up my mind not to use it at all. Now that I look over the score, I find it appearing more often than in any score I have ever written."

The charm of the song and of Liat's gestures should not blind the viewer to the fact that Bloody Mary is trying to inveigle (perhaps "pimping" is too strong a word) Cable into marrying her daughter—there is a method to her gladness. Evidently, the number worked in at least one case; during the West End run of the show, Betta St. John fell in love with her British Cable, Peter Grant. Dear reader, she married him, and left show business. (St. John's understudy, Chin Yu, married her Cable as well.) As Bloody Mary would say, "Is good idea—you like?"

PAGE 135: Betta St. John as Liat, Muriel Smith as Bloody Mary, and Peter Grant as Joe in the Drury Lane production, 1951. St. John and Grant would eventually marry.

OPPOSITE: John Kerr, Juanita Hall, and France Nuyen talk "happy" while trying to match the underwater location shots of the previous scene.

RIGHT: Nuyen had no previous theatrical or cinematic experience before perfectly embodying the image of exotic desire in the movie.

INTERMISSION:
THOUGHTS ON *SOUTH PACIFIC*

It took a lot of guts to open an American musical of the post-war era in a foreign language. When the curtain went up on *South Pacific* in April 1949, it must have baffled New York audiences to hear two schoolchildren singing a song in French. Wasn't the American musical created to connect immediately with its audience?

Rodgers and Hammerstein were acutely aware of what one might call the orchestration of a musical; not the actual arrangement of the musical instruments in the pit but the flow of a musical, how it reveals its component parts to an audience, its architecture. In starting *South Pacific* in another language, they were telling the audience that this show was all about language, translation, and how one culture communicates with another when nothing but obstacles stand in the way.

From the beginning of their collaboration on the show, before even Joshua Logan was involved as coauthor, Rodgers and Hammerstein knew they had a symphony of musical "languages" in the source material. As Rodgers wrote in the *New York Herald Tribune*:

> Emile de Becque, for example, is an expatriated Frenchman, and I tried to invest his songs with his personality—romantic, powerful, and not too involved. Nellie Forbush is a Navy nurse direct from a small town in Arkansas. Her musical and cultural background would have been confined to the radio, a certain number of movies, and perhaps that one trip to Chicago where she saw a touring musical comedy. In the whole score, there are two songs that could even remotely be considered "native." These are sung by a Tonkinese woman, and here I made no attempt to be authentic or realistic. The music is simply my impression of the woman and her surroundings in the same sense that a painter might give you the impression of a bowl of flowers rather than try to provide a photographic representation.

The score is nothing if not a series of separate "voices," much as Rodgers described. Hammerstein reinforces the point on Nellie's first entrance: "Why, I'm speechless!," she tells Emile—she must discover throughout the course of the musical *how* to speak to the man she loves. The first scene between Emile and Nellie on his plantation is a cultural transaction—each tries to help the other find the right way to communicate his or her thoughts. Emile makes several minor malapropisms and Nellie admits that, with the exception of conjugating a few verbs, she cannot speak his language. Even the "Twin Soliloquies" keeps their spoken thoughts encased in amber—they communicate most forcibly without speaking; audience members vividly remember Mary Martin and Ezio Pinza raising their brandy snifters together while gazing at each other as the height of 1940s romantic sensuality. After Nellie exits the first scene, Emile reverts to singing in French with his two children, indicating a linguistic chasm that will be difficult for Nellie to cross, which becomes a metaphor for a far wider cultural abyss that she will encounter later in the musical.

In the next scene, Rodgers and Hammerstein provide the musical equivalent of an amphibious American assault with the heavily aggressive chant of the Seabees: "Bloody Mary is the girl I love—Now ain't that too damn bad!" By using "ain't," "damn," "Pepsodent," and "DiMaggio" right off the bat, as it were, Hammerstein tossed several purely American words and phrases into the island paradise of Espiritu Santo. When Bloody Mary herself appears, she haphazardly purloins her own Americanisms: "Send home Chicago," "Chipskate!" "Droopy-drawers!" (In the Michener tale, she was particularly adept at appropriating the vilest of American curse words.) But as a shrewd businesswoman, Bloody Mary knows she has to barter between two cultures—Tonkinese and American—and that the best way to get what you want is to learn your opponent's language.

As the story unfolds further (and as Josh Logan contributes more to the collaboration), the notion of translation becomes more integral to the plot. Emile de Becque is sought out by Cable, Captain Brackett, and Ensign Harbison because he knows how to "read" the nearby Solomon Islands. Nellie informs Cable that her own mother "makes a big thing out of two people having different backgrounds:"

> For instance, if the man like symphony music and the girl likes Dinah Shore—and he reads Marcel Proust and she doesn't read anything . . .

Although Nellie claims her mother's perceptions are wrong, she decides to break off her relationship with Emile (who, presumably,

PAGE 138: The end of the first scene: De Becque embraces his beloved children, Ngana and Jerome, the products of a marriage to a Polynesian woman.

ABOVE: A universal language, underscored by cognac.

OPPOSITE: Lt. Cable, photographed here from the wings, thinking perhaps of the girl back home, while the girl right there, Liat, thinks only of him.

reads Proust) because, as she sings, "If the man don't understand you/ If you fly on different beams," you have to wash that man right outa your hair. The brassy jitterbug dance break in the song, where the nurses chime in, sounds like a pugnacious affirmation of American values sung by girls who like Dinah Shore. (In fact, Dinah Shore herself sang, "I'm Gonna Wash That Man Right Outa My Hair" quite well in Frank Sinatra's 1963 Reprise Musical Repertory Theatre recording.)

When Emile arrives on the scene he recognizes Nellie's tune immediately: "Is it a new American song?" He goes on to articulate the difference between American songs and European songs—the difference between Dinah Shore and Maurice Chevalier: "It is strange with your American songs. In all of them one is either desirous to get rid of one's lover, or one weeps for a man one cannot have. . . . I like a song that says 'I love you and you love me. . . . And isn't that fine?'" He manages to bring Nellie close enough to him that she sings several lines of his reprise to "Some Enchanted Evening"—she is beginning to sing his "language."

In the meantime, Lieutenant Cable is being seduced by the musical language of Bali Ha'i. His arrival on the island is heralded by a reprise of the song, this time sung in French by the sequestered native girls, French girls, and nuns who inhabit the island. French is the only non-Polynesian language that Liat can speak and when Cable first meets her, his ability to articulate his feelings is severely hampered by the fact that he can only speak "un peu" of French; he must resort to a more universal language. When he and Liat arise from their post-coital reverie, his highly poetic aria "Younger Than Springtime" makes no concession to the language barrier between them, but she ostensibly grasps the intensity of his romantic ardor. (In an earlier version, when Cable finished singing "Suddenly Lucky," he asked Liat, "Did you understand any of that?" "No," she replied, in what amounts to a monologue for Liat, "But pretty.")

Back on Espiritu Santo, Nellie has acquiesced to Emile's invitation to a dinner party; the departing guests convey their thanks to Emile in French. By now, Nellie is enchanted by the sophistication and exoticism of the party and of Emile's lifestyle: "Oh, it's so different from *Little Rock!*" She is so convinced that they have so "very much in common" that she can sing with him, in harmony, a reprise to "A Cockeyed Optimist"—in fact, the reprise is the height of their emotional harmony thus far in the show. But that bubble is immediately burst by Emile's revelation about his two children and their Polynesian mother. Once again, Nellie is rendered speechless by these cultural barriers: "And their mother . . . was a . . . was . . . a . . ." In Michener's tale, she could find the word quite easily— "nigger"—and in an earlier draft of the musical, she is able to say "colored." But in the final version of the musical, she can say nothing, she can sing nothing—she can only tell Emile that she loves him as she apologetically dashes off, leaving him alone to contemplate the chasm that has just opened between them.

In Act Two, Rodgers and Hammerstein give the audience a dash of good ol' American show business with the base's Thanksgiving Follies, which is, in its own way, a rather ingenious

ABOVE: Hands across the table; after an evening of rhapsodic singing,
the beginning of this new relationship will start in silence.

way of recreating American culture out of the found objects of the South Pacific—coconut brassieres, skirts made out of comic books— it is the most successful attempt at cultural translation we have seen so far in the musical. Perhaps inspired by that, Bloody Mary tries once again to seal the most important deal of her career: the marriage of her daughter to a handsome American lieutenant. In order for the spell to work, he must banish all thoughts of Philadelphia and think of all the island pleasures he will enjoy with Liat. Since their respective cultures are too far apart, she convinces them to speak their own language—"happy talk." Unfortunately, this utopian way of communication cannot hold up to the rigors of reality. Immediately following the song, Cable realizes he has ventured too far and has too much to lose; he rejects Liat as his wife and Bloody Mary rejects him as a "stingy bastard." It calls to mind Shakespeare's *The Tempest*, another island tale in which the native creature Caliban rejects his "civilized" master Prospero, saying "You taught me language; and my profit on't/Is, I know how to curse."

The next dramatic song is all about teaching. Nellie tells Emile that her prejudice is "emotional. This is something that is born in me." "What makes her talk like that?," asks Emile of Cable. Cable responds that people have to be taught their hatred and fear. As if shaking off his own hatred and fear, he tells Emile after the song that "if I get out of this thing alive . . . I'm coming here. All I care about is right here." Alas, the story of our characters in *South Pacific* does not allow Joe Cable to get out alive, so we never know if he would have been able to make good on his promise. As Cable's partner in the reconnaissance mission, de Becque's own survival is in question; Captain Brackett tries to assure Nellie of his chances by appropriating a phrase of her own: "He's okay . . . he's a wonderful guy." Nellie, according to the stage direction, "can only make an inarticulate sound of assent."

In the musical's concluding scene, Nellie makes an attempt to get acquainted with Emile's children as the sun sets in the distance, silhouetting the American embarkation for Operation Alligator. She is determined to communicate with the children in their own language, even though she is concerned that they will laugh at her French accent. (In fact, Jerome teaches Nellie a thing or two about American aircraft.) When she gamely starts to sing their song in French, Emile appears behind her and finishes her song. It seems that only when Nellie can courageously cross over into another culture can she earn her happy ending—complete with the return from certain death of her true love. Emile picks up her song, as the children join him, putting on

a brave face that nothing dangerous has ever happened to him or to his relationship with Nellie. Life can now continue, and it does, subtly. As he sits down to the table, while the children drink their soup, he and Nellie clasp each other's hands under the dining table. As "Some Enchanted Evening" swells from the orchestra, the curtain falls (on the final syllable of "*eve*ning," according to the stage manager's script).

In the first draft of the final scene, Emile, overcome with hunger, grabbed the ladle from the soup tureen, but Nellie silently made him sit down and be served—civilized society, after all. But, in the end, the final tableau created by Rodgers, Hammerstein, and Logan confounded as many conventions as the opening tableau did. Emile and Nellie do not join together in a rousing harmonized reprise of "Some Enchanted Evening" (although many viewers expect them to do so, because that is how the original cast album ended). Instead, they are joined together in another language that is successfully employed throughout the musical—silence. Compromise and collaboration can begin only when both sides stop forcing their language on the other. It is most telling that, in the final scene, not only does Nellie embrace Emile's language, he embraces her "first" language in the musical—her "speechless"-ness.

The idea of breaking down barriers and building new relationships was of paramount concern for the creators of the musical and for Hammerstein in particular. Across the globe, the world of the late 1940s had been drawn into a new map, with previous allies transmuted into enemies. The city of Berlin, for example, had been drawn into a quadrant with each sector speaking a different language. In America, the country was still trying to assimilate the seismic changes following the World War II. Only ten months before *South Pacific* opened, President Truman signed Executive Order 9981, which effectively ended segregation in the United States Armed Forces (the order was met with resistance by Army brass who declared that it was not the Army's place to conduct "social experiments" and so the order was not completely effected until 1953). By 1949, America had its first public glimpse of the House Un-American Activities Committee and its attempts to segregate United States citizens into two opposing ideological camps. For Rodgers, Hammerstein, and Logan, it was not a time to emphasize, let alone celebrate, our differences. Through the use of words and music, they hoped to unite audiences in the dream of a common language; in their cockeyed optimism, they appealed to what Abraham Lincoln called "the better angels of our nature."

HONEY BUN

Even when they're stuck in the middle of war, sometimes musical comedy types just wanna have fun. The Thanksgiving Follies that opens the second act of *South Pacific* is a completely original invention on the parts of Rodgers, Hammerstein, and Logan. (The timing of the Follies plays a little havoc with the historical reality—Operation Galvanic, the actual "Operation Alligator" occurred right before Thanksgiving, 1943.) Still, it's a shrewd way to introduce some musical comedy levity into a dark and emotionally trying Act Two. It also allows some of the supporting characters, such as Captain Brackett, to take center stage and remind the audience (watching both on the island of Espiritu Santo in 1943 and on Broadway in 1949) what they're fighting for:

> Up to now our side has been having the hell beat out of it in two hemispheres and we're not going to get to go home until that situation is reversed. It may take a long time before we can get any big operation under way, so it's things like this, like this show tonight that keep us going.

The creative team indulged themselves in some good-natured silliness. Hammerstein himself taught Mary Martin a goofy clog dance he learned in the 1920s; Leland Hayward suggested that the Navy nurses' chorus "costumes" be constructed out of "found" objects such as comic books; and Rodgers got a chance to use the kind of cornball vaudeville music he pastiched for *Pal Joey*. And you can never beat the sight of a big lug sporting a cocoanut brassiere.

My doll is as dainty as a sparrow,
Her figure is something to applaud.
Where's she's narrow, she's narrow as an arrow
And she's broad where a broad should be broad!

A hundred and one
Pounds of fun—
That's my little Honey Bun!
Get a load of Honey Bun tonight!

I'm speakin' of my
Sweetie Pie,
Only sixty inches high—
Ev'ry inch is packed with dynamite!

Her hair is blond and curly,
Her curls are hurly-burly,
Her lips are pips!
I call her hips:
"Twirly"
And "Whirly."

She's my baby,
I'm her Pap!
I'm her booby,
She's my trap!
I am caught and I don't wanta run
'Cause I'm havin' so much fun with Honey Bun!

ACT II - THANKSGIVING FOLLIES UNIT

PAGE 145: Mary Martin and Ray Walston reverse genders for some spirited horseplay in the Drury Lane production, 1951.

OPPOSITE, TOP: The cast of the Prince of Wales production, January 1988, joins together for a very American Thanksgiving Follies. Nellie Forbush, as played by actress Gemma Craven, can be seen as the Statue of Liberty.

OPPOSITE, BOTTOM: Michael Yeargan's clever design for the Follies, to be used in the Lincoln Center Theater revival, 2008. Notice the use of the official Seabee logo.

ABOVE: The pre-show: a group of nurses put together a chorus line the best they can. London, 1951.

RIGHT: A face only a mother could love: Myron McCormick, Broadway, 1949.

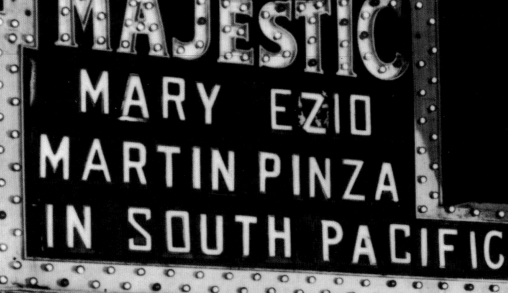

PART THREE:
COMING SOON TO A THEATER NEAR YOU

CHAPTER NINE
1950–1957

T he clamor for *South Pacific* tickets went into overdrive as soon as the late editions hit the streets on the evening of April 7. Rarely in the history of Broadway had a pair of tickets been in such demand. Scalpers were getting up to $500 for a pair of orchestra seats that had been bought for $6.00 each. A story circulated around town that one woman showed up to the box office for an evening performance to return one of her tickets because her husband had died. When the box office clerk kindly suggested she might bring a friend instead, she replied. "I can't. They're all at the funeral."

The mood was anything but funereal among the production staff. *South Pacific* made its money back by Labor Day, only six months after opening. Rodgers, Hammerstein, Logan, and Hayward were barraged by requests for house seats and many worthy friends and patrons had to be turned away or given seats months beyond their initial requests. Mary Martin did not even have two pairs of seats to give her son when he and some chums came to town; she told them to wait in line at the box office at six in the morning. As Hammerstein wrote to Logan, who had taken a month-long vacation after the opening, "The news from here is better than good. The advance hovers somewhere between $400,000 and $500,000. The audience hovers around the chandeliers throughout most of the performance and Pinza continues to hover over Mary Martin to everyone's delight and perhaps his own private frustration."

There were also scores of requests for benefit performances, so many that, early on, the production team took the strict party line that, out of fairness, *South Pacific* would not play any benefit performances, not even for a charity that wanted to erect a memorial for fallen soldiers in the South Pacific. Hammerstein had to turn down a telegram request from Walter White, the head of the NAACP, for a performance to benefit the association's fortieth birthday; it broke his heart, for no other organization could have been a more fitting beneficiary of *South Pacific*'s message of tolerance. (The producers eventually decided to raffle off fourteen house seats for the benefit of the Damon Runyon Memorial Fund for Cancer Research rather than see the money go to ticket scalpers.) Hayward and his partners even refused a $350,000 offer to televise the show live for one evening, though that decision was a financial one—they thought they could make more money keeping it at the Majestic Theatre, and they were probably right.

South Pacific fever struck Manhattan—there were *South Pacific* lipsticks, scarves, neckties, even fake ticket stubs that people could leave on their coffee tables as status symbols. The music from the show emanated from every radio set, every dance band, and every lounge piano player in New York City and beyond. The original cast album was recorded by Columbia ten days after the premiere and became the most popular record of the late 1940s; it was the number 1 album in the country for 69 consecutive weeks and wound up staying on the charts for a total of 400 weeks.

Then the awards started rolling in. Although *South Pacific* opened in April 1949, it had to wait until the following spring to be considered for the Tony Awards. (This was good news for Cole Porter, whose *Kiss Me, Kate* had opened on December 30, 1948 and was therefore able to sweep the 1949 Tony Awards.) However, the next year, *South Pacific* set all sorts of records in the Tonys' brief history. Not only did the show win for Best Musical, Best Director, Best Libretto, Best Score, and Best Producers (there was no separate award then for "Best Lyrics"), all four musical acting awards went to members of the cast: Ezio Pinza and Mary Martin for leading performers, and Myron McCormick and Juanita Hall as supporting or featured performers. To this day, no other production—dramatic or musical—has swept those four categories.

Not content with winning all the major awards in the theatrical community, *South Pacific* muscled in on the literary community as well. On May 2, 1950, the Pulitzer Prize board gave its Drama award to Rodgers, Hammerstein, and Logan for *South Pacific*. It was the first time a literary work had ever been recognized twice with a Pulitzer—one for Michener's *Tales of the South Pacific* and a second for the musical adaptation. A Pulitzer Prize for a musical was nearly unheard of; only *Of Thee I Sing*, the 1931 musical satire by George S. Kaufman, Morrie Ryskind, and George and Ira Gershwin had won in the Drama category before and, even then, composer George Gershwin was left out of the award. The citation for *South Pacific* made Rodgers the first musical theater composer to win a Pulitzer Prize.

Rodgers had little time to enjoy his award; as co-producers, he and Hammerstein were up to their ears with a national tour and plans for London. The national tour was launched the week before the Pulitzer Prize announcement; it opened in Cleveland and visited 118 cities in America

PAGE 148: *Broadway's biggest hit of the post-war era. The Majestic would eventually be the site of Broadway's all-time champ, The Phantom of the Opera, for two decades and beyond. . .*

PAGES 150–151: *In 1954, all four major television networks canceled their programming for a tribute to Rodgers and Hammerstein sponsored by General Foods. Here, at the curtain call, are Hammerstein, Mary Martin (she was the hostess for the evening), and Rodgers, center. They are surrounded by children from The King and I, as well as Tony Martin, Rosemary Clooney, Ed Sullivan, Ezio Pinza, Gordon Macrae (partial views), Groucho Marx, Patricia Morison, and ventriloquist dummy Charlie McCarthy.*

OPPOSITE, TOP: *At the Columbia Records studio, Martin, Rodgers, and Pinza listen intently to the playback*

OPPOSITE, BOTTOM: *The same session; Rodgers and Barbara Luna, who is probably wondering why the sky is filled with music.*

ABOVE: *In 1950, when all the Tony Awards were given out; South Pacific received more than half of them. Here is Helen Hayes (who starred in Happy Birthday, a play produced by Rodgers and Hammerstein and directed by Josh Logan), presenting awards to Logan, Myron McCormick, Leland Hayward, Rodgers, and Hammerstein.*

before winding down in 1955. The leads were Janet Blair, Richard Eastham (Pinza's understudy in New York), and Ray Walston as Billis, a role he would repeat in London and in the film version. The demand for the Cleveland engagement was so immense—250,000 requests for only 48,000 available seats—that the box office had to close for three weeks to handle the mail. In 1951, a scaled-down version toured army installations in Korea—Rodgers and Hammerstein insisted that the officers and the enlisted men be allowed to sit together.

At the Majestic, Mary Martin appeared to be having the time of her life; certainly it was the highlight of her career. She was adored by her fellow castmates and never missed a performance, washing her hair eight shows a week. Across the backstage hall, in the other star dressing room, it was a different story. Ezio Pinza had become a media super-star. The fifty-eight-year-old singer was acclaimed as the surprise sex symbol of his day—critic George Jean Nathan wrote that "Pinza has taken the place of Hot Springs, Saratoga, and hormone injections for all the other old boys"—and one New York politician wooed his much younger fiancée by crooning "Some Enchanted Evening" in front of the newsreel cameras. The attention was just what Pinza was waiting for; three days after the opening of *South Pacific*, he signed an agreement with Metro-Goldwyn-Mayer to make movies as soon as his one-year contract with the show expired. Nothing could make him change his mind and the minute his time was up, he zoomed to California so fast it made heads spin. During the run, Pinza had a difficult time adjusting to speaking lines on stage week after week and developed various colds and voice ailments. Audiences were none too happy about his frequent absences, and for the rest of his life, Rodgers resented Pinza's evacuation to the West Coast.

While all this was going on, James Michener was flying past the West Coast and on to Asia. The success of the musical adaptation and his second book had turned him into a citizen of the world and one of America's greatest experts on Asian culture. He visited Hawaii and took copious notes for a historical novel about that territory; returned to the South Pacific to write a series of articles about how life had changed there; and was beginning a novel called *Sayonara* about a group of American GIs in Japan during the Korean War. His peripatetic spirit was taking him far beyond the world of New York's Theater District, but he never forgot the financial freedom that *South Pacific* gave him, nor the back-stage operatic singalongs he had with his idol, Ezio Pinza, nor the comradeship of Rodgers and Hammerstein. While tooling around the Solomon Islands in early 1951, he sent a letter to them in New York: "Having seen the hot islands again, *South Pacific* seems more real and natural than when I was comparing it to my recollection. I don't recall one phony touch." Michener also kept up with Joshua Logan, and when he finished *Sayonara*, he contacted Logan about turning it into a musical. That never happened, but when it was made into a film in 1957, it was directed by Logan, with Irving Berlin contributing the title song over the credits.

At the same time, Logan's collaboration with Rodgers and Hammerstein was undergoing a strange passive aggression. They took great exceptions to the changes that Logan had made in the national tour of *South Pacific* and browbeat him into restaging it exactly as it had been on Broadway. The tension only increased when Logan flew to London in October 1951 to see how the Drury Lane production of *South Pacific* was progressing under the supervision of Jerry Whyte, a glorified stage manager for the Rodgers and Hammerstein firm. Mary Martin was reprising her role as Nellie opposite Wilbur Evans, and she practically recoiled from Logan when he greeted her backstage—evidently she had been warned about Logan's tinkering with the national tour. "No changes, Josh," she told him. Martin was in a vulnerable position—she had last appeared in London in 1947, starring in the first musical to open at Drury Lane after World War II, *Pacific 1860* by Noël Coward, and it had not gone well for either of them. And since *Oklahoma!* had been the box office phenomenon

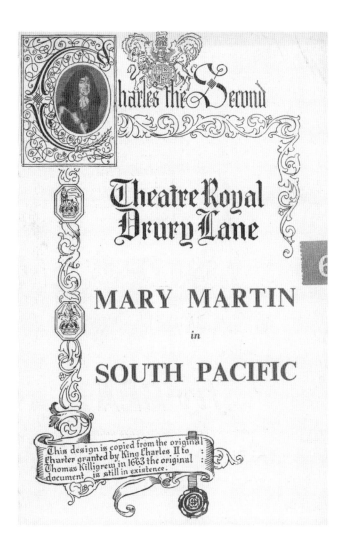

TOP, LEFT AND RIGHT: Quick—name two musicals that Mary Martin performed in London with the word "Pacific" in the title! Well, one you already know; the other was Pacific 1860, written by Noël Coward. A musical romance set on a mythical island, the 1947 extravaganza reopened Drury Lane after the war and was a failure.

RIGHT: Martin gamely returns to the scene of the crime, marching jauntily up the steps to the Theatre Royal, Drury Lane, 1951.

ABOVE: Backstage after the triumphant opening at Drury Lane, on November 1, 1951, Martin is hugged by her son, actor Larry Hagman, who also had a small part in the show.

OPPOSITE: Ezio Pinza did not rejoin Martin for the London version; here, her Emile is the dependable American baritone, Wilbur Evans.

of the post-war West End world, the keen anticipation for *South Pacific* only added to her anxiety.

Logan was able to reassure her and jolly her up; as a result, *South Pacific* opened on November 1 at the Drury Lane and was all that Londoners had hoped it would be. London critics, perhaps skeptical about all the pre-opening frenzy, were not overly kind. "We got a 42nd Street Madame Butterfly, the weakest of all the Hammerstein-Rodgers musicals," wrote the London *Daily Express*. "The play moved so slowly between its songs that it seemed more like *South Soporific*," commented the Daily Mail. Yet the frequently irascible Kenneth Tynan, at the dawn of his career as a drama critic, wrote for the *Spectator*: "[It is] the first musical romance which was seriously involved in an adult subject . . . I have nothing to do but thank Logan, Rodgers and Hammerstein and climb up from my knees, a little cramped from the effort of typing in such an unusual position."

The critical community seemed eager to move on to more serious fare—"Well, it's happened. *South Pacific* has arrived at Drury Lane and we ought now be able to turn our attention to such minor matters as the issue of world war and peace," wrote one columnist. Still, it ran for nearly 800 performances, a huge number for the West End, and long enough for a young actor named Sean Connery to take over the chorus role of a Seabee. (Larry Hagman began his acting career playing a small part in the chorus, on stage with his mother.)

In the meantime, despite whatever misgivings Rodgers and Hammerstein had about Logan's restagings, they wanted to work with him again. They sent him a play to consider as a musical—a dramatic adaptation of some Yiddish stories by Sholem Aleichem called *Tevya's Daughters*. Logan could not see anything dramatic, let alone musical, in the material, so he passed on the project (more than a decade later, of course, and in other hands it became *Fiddler on the Roof*). Rodgers and Hammerstein then offered Logan the directorial reigns, as well as coauthorship, of their next show, *The King and I*, but Logan sat on his decision for a long time, and even made some suggestions, before he ultimately declined; he had been burnt so badly from his contractual treatment by Rodgers and Hammerstein on *South Pacific* that he did not have the heart to go forward (and perhaps he wanted to punish them somehow).

The three men went their several ways; Logan succeeded on the dramatic stage directing new work by

William Inge, while Rodgers and Hammerstein had a smash hit with *The King and I* and a mild disappointment with the backstage musical comedy *Me and Juliet*. Toward the end of 1953, Logan tried to interest the team in a new musical based on a trilogy of French films by Marcel Pagnol. Rodgers and Hammerstein loved the material, but once again their business instincts took center stage; they refused to share a producing credit with David Merrick, the St. Louis lawyer who had optioned the material in the first place, and walked away from the project. In the first week of January 1954, *South Pacific*'s Broadway run had finally come to an end, after 1,925 performances, having played for an estimated 3,500,000 paying customers. But even after the show ultimately transferred to the Broadway Theatre towards the end of its run, the curtain literally never came down—it was left up out of respect for the show and its five years of triumph. In November of 1954, Logan finally opened the Pagnol project, now called *Fanny*, and it was like a family reunion. The show starred Ezio Pinza and William Tabbert, and the ingénue was played by a very young Florence Henderson, who would go on to play Nellie in the 1967 Music Theater of Lincoln Center revival of *South Pacific*. Pinza's movie career never took off, so he was happy to be back in a hit Broadway show; but he would suffer several strokes during the run and passed away in 1957.

    South Pacific itself never went away. There was always a stock or summer production of it somewhere (Martin took up the sailor suit in 1957 for a brief California tour; Barbara Luna, the original Ngana, was promoted to Liat). During the second week of September 1957, the show had another brief rendezvous with destiny. While *South Pacific* was playing a stock production at Long Island's Westbury Music Fair, the Governor of Arkansas had called in the National Guard to prevent nine black students from enrolling at the all-white Little Rock Central High. That week, whenever the Music Fair's Nellie announced she was from Little Rock, she was greeted with boos from the largely suburban audience. Clearly that would not do for "our heroine." Logan refused to change the name of the town, so a curtain speech was made, asking for the audience's, well, tolerance. Logan could not have been more pleased. As he told the press, "It shows the audience at once that Nellie is from the most prejudiced and ignorant part of our country. The controversy validates our story."

ABOVE: *During the London success, a couple of hit songs were released on 45s. Andrew Lloyd Webber's father, William, predicted that after Londoners heard "Some Enchanted Evening," the birthrate in England would start to soar.*

OPPOSITE: *Fanny, a musical version of Marcel Pagnol's film trilogy, was turned into a musical by Harold Rome in 1954. Josh Logan directed and the cast included William Tabbert, as well as the young Florence Henderson (left) and Ezio Pinza, in his last stage role.*

PAGE 161: *William Tabbert, chiselled integrity, self-righteousness, and self-loathing.*

YOU'VE GOT TO BE CAREFULLY TAUGHT

You've got to be taught to hate and fear,
You've got to be taught from year to year,
It's got to be drummed in your dear little ear—
You've got to be carefully taught!

You've got to be taught to be afraid
Of people whose eyes are oddly made,
And people whose skin is a different shade—
You've got to be carefully taught.

You've got to be taught before it's too late,
Before you are six or seven or eight,
To hate all the people your relatives hate—
You've got to be carefully taught!
You've got to be carefully taught!

CHAPTER TEN
1958

Rodgers and Hammerstein each had terrible experiences in Hollywood. They were determined not to have them together. After *Oklahoma!* became a smash hit on stage, they retained the film rights by buying out the Theatre Guild and holding on to the rights until they found the best way to translate the musical to the screen; ultimately they set up their own film company and installed themselves as executive producers. They became enthusiastic about a widescreen process called Todd-AO, which they thought deepened and broadened the screen picture beyond the usual film musical. The result was a handsome, if not particularly limber, version of *Oklahoma!* in 1955, which made more than $2 million in profit in its first domestic release alone. If *Oklahoma!* was not great cinema, it was at least under Rodgers and Hammerstein's control, which is more than could be said for the 1956 movie versions of *Carousel* and *The King and I*. They were also big moneymakers but, due to previous contracts, they were made by 20th Century Fox without creative involvement by Rodgers and Hammerstein.

South Pacific, however, was too important to them. It also cried out for a particularly broad cinematic canvas, and Rodgers and Hammerstein wanted its look and mood to be carefully controlled. After the movie rights were sold to 20th Century Fox for $1,250,000, they decided to go with the Todd-AO brand of cinematography again and to set up a private corporation to produce the movie with Fox. After some hemming and hawing, they hired Josh Logan to direct the movie. In the years since *South Pacific* opened on Broadway, Logan had considerable success directing two movie adaptations of the work of William Inge, *Picnic* and *Bus Stop*. When the offer came his way to film *South Pacific*, he was in pre-production for *Sayonara* with Marlon Brando, which went on to win two Academy Awards. Logan felt he could stand by his movie career, and when he was offered less than he thought he should accept to transfer *South Pacific* to the screen, he demanded part of the box office profits. Rodgers and Hammerstein agreed and set up a generous profit-sharing arrangement with Logan that made up for the contract he was forced to sign on the stage version.

During the movie's preproduction phase, Rodgers had taken ill and was, for all intent and purposes, not much involved with shooting the picture. Hammerstein was, however, and he appeared to love every minute of it, especially the location scouting. In the fall of 1956, he had gone to Australia to give a few speeches, attend a benefit screening of *The King and I,* and then traveled around the South Pacific, looking for the right scenery for Bali Ha'i and the navy base locations that would make up most of the movie. "Kauai is the island for us," he cabled back to Logan, enamored with the magical island in Hawaii that had only been used once before in a picture, a silly Tahitian musical starring Esther Williams called *Pagan Love Song* in 1950. The line producer for Fox, Buddy Adler, and the coproducer, George Skouras had managed to secure the cooperation of the navy and the marines, which saved a lot of money; and the location filming was timed to coincide with some naval war games, which made for a particularly effective "Operation Alligator".

Casting would be crucial, as always, but the production crew had to start afresh. Pinza had died earlier that year (he would have loved to star in the movie) and Mary Martin was simply too old for the widescreen lens. Logan very much wanted Elizabeth Taylor for the part of Nellie, but when she auditioned for Rodgers, she froze up and could barely croak out a note; no amount of Logan's pleading could change Rodgers' mind. Doris Day presented herself as an obvious Nellie Forbush, but Logan was never enthusiastic. When Day refused to sing at a dinner party at Rosalind Russell's home, where Logan was in attendance, he knew his instincts were right—they would never have gotten along. He was somewhat intrigued by Mitzi Gaynor, a perky twenty-six-year-old who had enlivened some dull musicals in the early 1950s. When the producer Arthur Hornblow told Logan that, if he sat on her and carefully managed her forced sunniness, Gaynor would work very well, he cast her and was thoroughly pleased with her work.

Casting Gaynor's co-star proved more difficult. Rodgers had cast the darkly handsome Italian actor Rossano Brazzi after hearing him sing "Some Enchanted Evening" at a dinner party at Dorothy Sarnoff's house (what is it with all these dinner party auditions?). Brazzi had starred as another Continental charmer opposite Katharine Hepburn in the movie *Summertime* (which Rodgers would eventually adapt with Stephen Sondheim into the 1964 musical, *Do I Hear a*

PAGE 164: *Mitzi Gaynor and Rossano Brazzi embrace in the movie version, 1958.*

PAGES 166–167: *Two "vets" from South Pacific reunite for the movie; Juanita Hall from Broadway and Ray Walston from the road and the London productions.*

ABOVE: *Pardon my sarong: Esther Williams stars in Pagan Love Song, the first movie to be shot on location on Kauai, 1950.*

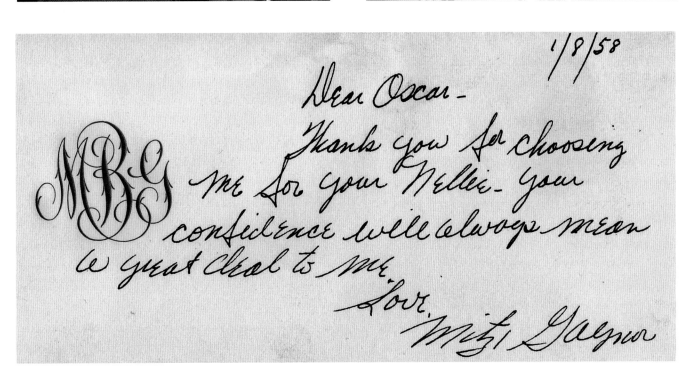

1/8/58

Dear Oscar –
Thank you for choosing
me for your Nellie. Your
confidence will always mean
a great deal to me.
Love,
Mitzi Gaynor

TOP, RIGHT: Mitzi Gaynor was an up-and-coming actress with minimal musical film experience when she was catapulted to the lead in the movie. Her youth and joy impressed the producers.

TOP, LEFT: She confers with Oscar Hammerstein, to whom she sent the thank-you note, bottom.

TOP AND LEFT: Promotional material for the movie. In the UK, the movie was particularly beloved and the soundtrack album for South Pacific remains the most successful in British history, landing at Number One for 185 weeks—three years!—and staying on the charts for a total of 313 weeks.

OPPOSITE: Hard to know if Rossano Brazzi was thinking about the super-imposed Mitzi Gaynor or Giorgio Tozzi who, to Brazzi's dismay, dubbed his singing. Despite the infamous color tinting in the movie of South Pacific, one will never see it in the production stills—those are always shot separately by studio photographers.

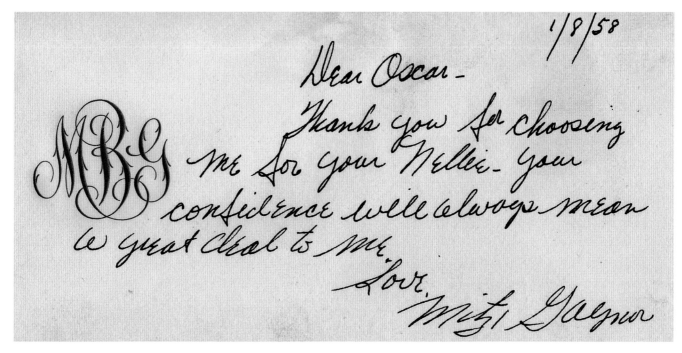

1/8/58

Dear Oscar —
Thanks you for choosing
me for your Nellie. Your
confidence will always mean
a great deal to me.
Love,
Mitzi Gaynor

TOP, RIGHT: Mitzi Gaynor was an up-and-coming actress with minimal musical film experience when she was catapulted to the lead in the movie. Her youth and joy impressed the producers.

TOP, LEFT: She confers with Oscar Hammerstein, to whom she sent the thank-you note, bottom.

Waltz?); Brazzi would go on to star as another Continental charmer in the movie of *The Light in the Piazza*, which Rodgers' grandson, Adam Guettel, would adapt as a musical in 2003) and seemed to fit the bill. However, by the time Brazzi reported for duty, Rodgers and Hammerstein decided he should be dubbed by opera singer Giorgio Tozzi (who even received an on-screen credit for his voice). Brazzi's *amour propre* was thoroughly damaged by this turnabout and he sulked mightily while blowing the lip-synching to Tozzi's playback on location. He exploded with fury that "Diss god-damn cheap shit voice, I cannot sing to it." Once Logan tactfully explained that a lot of money was being wasted while Brazzi was nursing his ego, Brazzi bucked up and finished the picture professionally, if not enthusiastically.

Dubbing seemed to be an omnipresent problem on the picture. The handsome young John Kerr as Joe Cable was dubbed by Bill Lee (who would later dub Christopher Plummer on *The Sound of Music*); even Juanita Hall, who had won the Tony on Broadway as Bloody Mary, was dubbed by Muriel Smith, who was one of the original "Carmen Jones" and had played Bloody Mary in London's West End. Out of the major leads, only Gaynor and Ray Walston, reprising Billis for the second time, sang their roles; the beautiful half-French, half-Chinese model France Nuyen, making her film debut, had little to say, anyway.

The movie remains a surprisingly faithful version of the stage musical; it is the only one of Rodgers and Hammerstein's shows to make it relatively intact to the screen (a few numbers are trimmed slightly). In fact, "My Girl Back Home" makes it into the movie, as a particularly effective duet between Cable and Nellie that nicely ties their stories together. ("Loneliness of Evening," an out-of-town casualty in 1949, creeps in as the text of a written note from Emile to Nellie.) Music supervisor and orchestrator Alfred Newman and music arranger Ken Darby enhance the musical score with all the lushness available to a 1950s studio orchestra. Logan had hired the distinguished Broadway playwright Paul Osborn to write the screenplay

and, other than screw up Hammerstein's carefully calibrated opening (the first fifteen minutes, perhaps under-standably in a movie, are "opened up" to show Cable flying to the island on a PBY, before landing on the beach to confront Bloody Mary), his adaptation keeps the salient points of the original while staying out of the way. The latter quarter of the movie, Emile and Cable's mission to Marie Louise Island and Billis' rescue, are nicely reimagined for the screen, and discerning viewers can catch a little sexual frisson between Commander Bill Harbison and Nellie Forbush, a holdover from one of Michener's stories.

Logan was one of the few directors given a chance to stage both an original play on Broadway and its movie version, so, in many ways, the movie remains a fair record of what worked at the Majestic Theatre. What is missing is a depth of visual field—Logan knows how to move things laterally, but with the exception of the rare shot of a jeep driving along a road in the distance behind Nellie seated in Emile's pagoda, for example, he does not quite exploit the visual canvas available to him. What Logan did bring to

ABOVE: On location in Kauai. The "Honey Bun" number, which Richard Rodgers thought was ludicrously overpopulated.

OPPOSITE, TOP: Josh Logan, shirtless himself for a change, directs Gaynor.

BOTTOM: An "opened-up" scene with the Seabee corps.

TOP AND LEFT: Promotional material for the movie. In the UK, the movie was particularly beloved and the soundtrack album for South Pacific remains the most successful in British history, landing at Number One for 185 weeks— three years!—and staying on the charts for a total of 313 weeks.

OPPOSITE: Hard to know if Rossano Brazzi was thinking about the super-imposed Mitzi Gaynor or Giorgio Tozzi who, to Brazzi's dismay, dubbed his singing. Despite the infamous color tinting in the movie of South Pacific, one will never see it in the production stills—those are always shot separately by studio photographers.

the film, to his everlasting regret, was a series of color filters, developed with the assistance of the director of photography, Leon Shamroy, to enhance the musical numbers. It was always Logan's contention that a movie musical should, in some way, capture those emotional and atmospheric changes that occur in a stage musical when the orchestra cues up for a song, the lights change color, and the spotlight focuses on the singer. Shamroy never thought the process would work, but the studio gave the idea the green light, saying the process could be reversed in post-production should it prove distracting. Hammerstein expressed his displeasure at the rushes quite clearly, but Logan and Shamroy persisted.

What transpired was that the studio decided that the reversal process was too expensive and time-consuming. Fox needed to release its $6,500,000 picture on schedule for mid-March 1958; it had been booked as a prestigious "road show" movie, with advance ticketing, an overture, and so on.

A delay would be impossible. Logan was stuck with a picture that was deeply flawed because of a technical mistake that overshadowed much of what was good about the film. Audiences didn't seem to mind; *South Pacific* brought in $17,000,000 on its domestic release, making it the third top-grossing movie of the 1950s. In England, they went absolutely mad for the picture. It was the greatest money earner in the United Kingdom until *Goldfinger* in 1963. At the Dominion Theatre in the West End, it made $1,500,000 in its first year; it went on to play at that theater for five years, making enough money at that one venue to cover the entire production costs of the movie.

When Logan visited London in the early 1960s, he used to apologize to the press and the British public for the wretched color filters that had ruined *South Pacific*, until one of the reporters said, "But, Mr. Logan, the *color* was what we *liked*."

THIS NEARLY WAS MINE

One dream in my heart,
One love to be living for,
One love to be living for—
This nearly was mine.

One girl for my dreams,
One partner in Paradise,
This promise of Paradise—
This nearly was mine.

Close to my heart she came,
Only to fly away,
Only to fly as day
Flies from moonlight!

Now, now I'm alone,
Still dreaming of Paradise.
Still saying that Paradise
Once nearly was mine.

So clear and deep are my fancies
Of things I wish were true,
I'll keep remembering evenings
I wish I'd spent with you.
I'll keep remembering kisses
From lips I'll never own
And all the lovely adventures
That we have never known.

One dream in my heart
One love to be living for,
One love to be living for—
This nearly was mine.

One girl for my dreams,
One partner in Paradise,
This promise of Paradise—
This nearly was mine.

Close to my heart she came,
Only to fly away,
Only to fly as day
Flies from moonlight!

Now… now I'm alone,
Still dreaming of Paradise,
Still saying that Paradise
Once nearly was mine.

Before *South Pacific* began its out-of-town tryout, Ezio Pinza had an eleven o'clock number in Act Two called "Now is the Time." His character was to sing it when he impulsively agrees to go with Cable on a secret espionage mission. It was very masculine, very decisive, and used up at least four minutes of Pinza's contractually allotted fifteen:

> Now!
> Now is the time,
> The time to act,
> No other time will do.
> Live and play your part
> And give away your heart
> And take what the world gives you.

Joshua Logan realized there was a major dramaturgical flaw to the whole thing: "If Cable and Emile were going on a mission to save Allied lives, why didn't they get a goddamn move on instead of standing and singing?" Logan, Rodgers, and Hammerstein quickly discussed an alternative and they arrived at the idea that the song could come out of Emile's sense of loss and despair at losing Nellie, bringing him to a kind of existential resolve that would culminate in volunteering for the mission. Rodgers asked for a title, perhaps a dummy title, anything to get him started. Someone shouted out "This nearly was mine." "That's it," said Rodgers, and within forty-eight hours, he and Hammerstein came back with a deep river of a song, a slow waltz filled with longing. It fit Pinza down to the ground and he adored singing it.

Today, the song is the show's "secret weapon," as Ted Chapin put it in the commentary for the film's 2006 DVD release. Everyone knows that "Some Enchanted Evening" is in the score, but most people forget about this song and are stunned by its beauty and power. When Brian Stokes Mitchell sang it at the 2005 concert at Carnegie Hall, he stopped the evening cold in its tracks.

According to Rodgers, the only person who never really liked the song was Hammerstein. He hated the use of the word "paradise" because he felt it was overused, rendered ineffectual by generations of songwriting hacks, but he was never able to come up with anything better. "Admittedly," wrote Rodgers in *Musical Stages*, "the word did convey exactly the way the character felt: he was close to paradise, whether Oscar liked it or not."

Ezio Pinza, great basso of opera, Broadway, and TV fame, is now starring in Broadway's smash musical hit, *Fanny*

THE GREAT **Ezio Pinza** SAYS OF KRAFT'S NEW ITALIAN DRESSING—

"Magnifico! It makes salads taste like they ought to!"

● This new Italian Dressing of Kraft's is a golden oil-and-vinegar dressing so unusual, so delightful, it will make your salads famous. Seasoned with rare herbs, fresh spices, and a touch of garlic, it's *fabulously* good. Wonderful, too, is the way Kraft Italian mixes. Oil and vinegar don't separate on the salad; the dressing clings to the greens so every morsel is deliciously coated. Try it soon!

KRAFT *Italian dressing*

Kraft NEW

PAGE 175: One of the few shots of Pinza in combat gear—after singing "This Nearly Was Mine," he was ready to go on a surveillance mission.

OPPOSITE: Pinza became a major theater superstar; here he lends his Mediterranean charm to salad dressing.

ABOVE: Pinza's real goal was to become a movie superstar—it never quite happened. Seen here with Paula Raymond, Pinza submits to a screen test for Mr. Imperium, which uses a tropical background and, coincidentally, refers to the title Mr. Ambassador, the unwritten stage show that led him to South Pacific.

RODGERS & HAMMERSTEIN'S
SOUTH
PACIFIC
DIRECTED BY BARTLETT SHER
LINCOLN CENTER THEATER

CHAPTER ELEVEN

THE TWENTY-FIRST CENTURY

A long with *South Pacific*, Rodgers and Hammerstein created *Oklahoma!*, *Carousel*, *The King and I*, and *The Sound of Music*, each beloved box-office bonanzas. In the twenty-first century those musicals were no different, no better than *South Pacific*, but, to paraphrase the *Wizard of Oz*, they have one thing that *South Pacific* hasn't got: a first-class Broadway revival. The path to that Broadway revival took nearly six decades.

After the movie version of *South Pacific* made its successful run at box offices all over the world, the four original collaborators, for the most part, went their separate ways. For Rodgers and Hammerstein, there would be one great project left together after 1958; the following year's Broadway success of *The Sound of Music*, which reunited them with Mary Martin and Leland Hayward. During the creation of that show, Hammerstein had become fatally ill with stomach cancer; he was able to attend—and tend to— the opening, but soon retired to his farm in Doylestown to live out his days. He was frequently visited by his neighbor, James Michener, and only a week or so before his death in August of 1960, Michener paid a last visit. Michener was about to play the part of the Professor in a local summer stock production of *South Pacific*. Hammerstein counseled him to take the job seriously and they joked about how the song "You've Got to be Carefully Taught" caused so much anxiety among certain viewers that, according to Hammerstein, "nobody wound up mentioning the ballads." The two men agreed that the rehearsals for *South Pacific* were "a golden time."

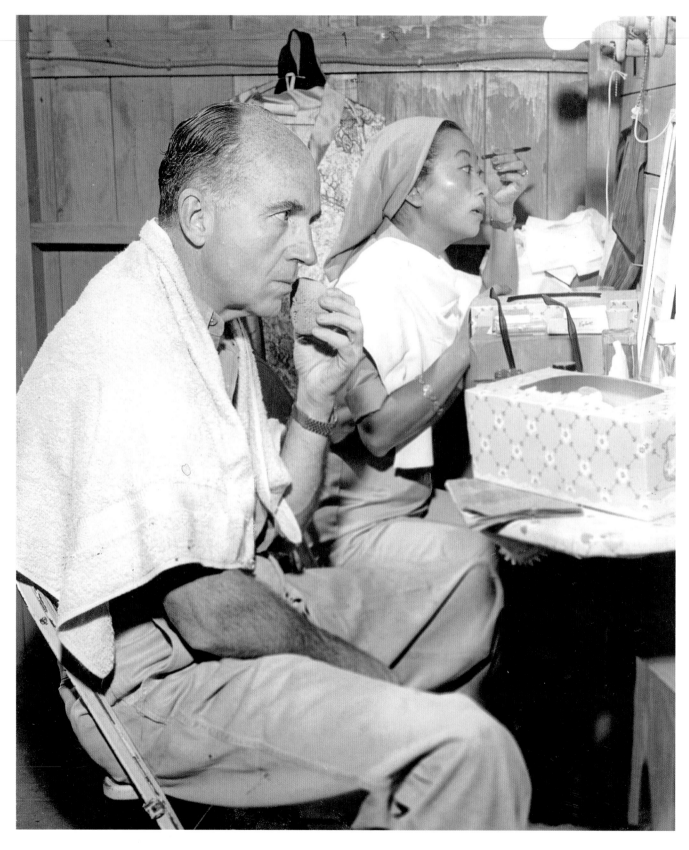

PAGE 178: James McMullan's joyous watercolor poster for the Lincoln Center Theater revival, 2008.

ABOVE: James Michener always loved the theater; South Pacific gave him a venue (and royalties). Here he makes up for the role of the Professor, expanded for him in a 1959 summer stock production in Lambertville, Bucks

County. His wife, Mari, is about to join him—as Bloody Mary?

OPPOSITE: Logan was a very loyal director, frequently teaming up with alumni from earlier productions. Here, in 1958, he directs the stage version of The World of Suzie Wong, starring France Nuyen. Her leading man is the young William Shatner.

By 1960, Michener was well on his way to becoming one of the most successful and prolific novelists of the twentieth century. His historical novel *Hawaii* had just been published (it would be made into a movie starring one of Rodgers and Hammerstein's favorite performers, Julie Andrews) and he was enjoying his marriage to his third wife, Mari Sabusawa, a second-generation Japanese American. Mari had been interned in a Japanese relocation camp in California during the World War II and was a major influence in expanding Michener's already broad horizons on racial tolerance. She forbade him to use the word "Japs" in front of her. With Mari, Michener became a world traveler, political activist, and philanthropist. In 1985, under the aegis of television's *60 Minutes*, he made a moving return to Espiritu Santo, where he was interviewed by Diane Sawyer about his time there during the war. By the time he passed away in 1997, Michener had written nearly forty books, which were read by millions of readers across the globe.

Richard Rodgers and Josh Logan were never able to return to the fond relationship they enjoyed in the early 1940s. Rodgers worked with several new collaborators on Broadway projects in the 1960s, while Logan spread his cinematic wings by directing the movie versions of two Lerner and Loewe musicals, *Camelot* and *Paint Your Wagon*. Although they were cordial socially, Logan was still stung by the royalty arrangement for *South Pacific* and frequently had to remind Rodgers (or his office) that his name had to appear alongside Oscar Hammerstein's in all programs and publicity for future productions. Rodgers, to his mind, had settled all that many years ago.

One of those productions was the first major revival of the show. Rodgers had been appointed president of an informal repertory musical theater at the new Lincoln Center. The Music Theater of Lincoln Center produced a version of *South Pacific* in 1967 starring Florence Henderson (who had been a very popular Maria in the national tour of *The Sound of Music*) and Giorgio Tozzi, who had provided Emile de Becque's singing voice in the 1958 film. Under the direction of Joe Layton, a frequent Rodgers collaborator, the production at the New York State Theatre featured a set by Fred Voelpel that came out over the orchestra pit (the orchestra players were placed backstage) with a false proscenium using over-scaled frangipani to frame the on-stage action. It was also the last major New York revival of their lifetimes; Rodgers would

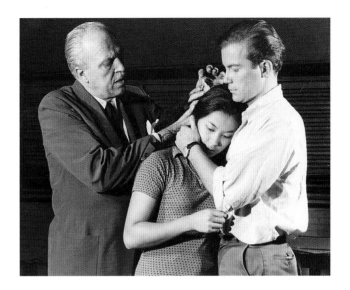

pass away in 1979, Logan in 1988. The only other significant revival was a commercial West End production at the Prince of Wales Theatre in January 1988. Here, the leads were the gamine Gemma Craven and Emile Belcourt (a Frenchman, finally!) as the romantic leads.

In 1986, the first inklings of a creative reimagining of *South Pacific* occurred in Henry Wood Hall in London. The year before, Leonard Bernstein had conducted his score to *West Side Story* as a studio recording for Deutsche Grammophon, featuring a battalion of opera singers and starring Kiri Te Kanawa and José Carreras. It was a phenomenal success and ushered in a slew of studio recordings in which opera (and movie) stars tackled the crown jewels of the musical theater canon. If any show deserved an operatic crossover, it was *South Pacific*, a major milestone in bringing opera singers to the legitimate stage. CBS/Sony brought Carreras and Te Kanawa back to the studio, under the baton of Broadway's most accomplished modern orchestrator, Jonathan Tunick, who conducted the fifty-plus members of the London Symphony Orchestra. Joining them were Mandy Patinkin as a febrile Lieutenant Cable and Sarah Vaughan, the diva of the jazz world, as a particularly languid Bloody Mary. The singing role of de Becque was written for a bass but Carreras is a tenor, so some of the music was transposed for his range (recordings have different rules than the theater). That did not stop the recording from becoming another hit in the crossover category; in the New York Times, Stephen Holden wrote that "the star of this *South Pacific* isn't any individual, but rather the score itself. . . [it] suggests an allegory of America emerging victoriously from the war."

When the fiftieth anniversary of the Broadway opening rolled around, it was celebrated with style. The Rodgers and Hammerstein Organization sponsored a series of events to remind the public how groundbreaking the original show was; there was a proclamation from New York's mayor, Rudolph Giuliani, as well as one from the mayor of Little Rock, Arkansas, and a special celebration on the stage of the Majestic, following a matinee of *The Phantom of the Opera*, which had been in residence there for more than a decade. More than twenty-five original cast members gathered at the Majestic, and for a special symposium at Symphony Space, a first and last reunion where members of the original cast—including Barbara Luna, Betta St. John, Don Fellows, and Richard Eastham (Pinza's understudy)—reminisced, accompanied by professional performers singing some of the score's highlights.

It was not until 2001, however, that a newly conceived production of *South Pacific* appeared on the stage—and that stage was the voluminous Olivier Theatre at London's Royal National Theatre. In the 1990s, several British directors, including Trevor Nunn and Nicholas Hytner, ordinarily at home with serious dramas, tried their hands at rethinking some of the major musicals of the American canon. The results—Hytner's *Carousel* and Nunn's *Oklahoma!*, for example—were often revelatory; in fact, both productions did so well at the box office that they later played on Broadway. Nunn, who was also the artistic director of the National, thought it was time to reexamine *South Pacific*. Ironically, while he was in preproduction, trying to create a context of a world at war for a 2001 audience, the tragic events of September 11, 2001, occurred. It was a resonance that profoundly affected Nunn; in the liner notes for the RNT cast album, he wrote that Rodgers, Hammerstein, and Logan "were presenting a world in the balance, a future full of uncertainty and pervasive knowledge of decisive battles about to be fought. . . . In the future we are facing, we can be in no doubt about the need for such determined optimism in our lives." Nunn's production marshaled the full force of the National's resources; newsreels, jeeps, a complex stage design, and a cast of thirty-seven. He also borrowed some things from the movie and tinkered with the show's structure, placing Nellie and Emile's first scene after the introduction of Bloody Mary, Billis, and Cable. Several songs deleted from Broadway were restored, mostly in the Act Two. Nunn's

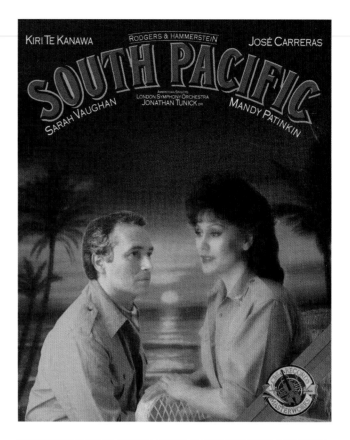

TOP: José Carreras and Kiri Te Kanawa in the successful 1986 studio recording.

BOTTOM: Richard Kiley and Meg Bussert team up for a Los Angeles production in 1985; it never made it to Broadway.

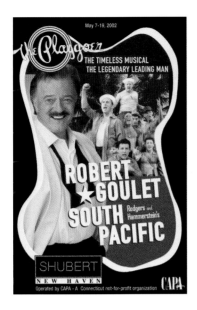

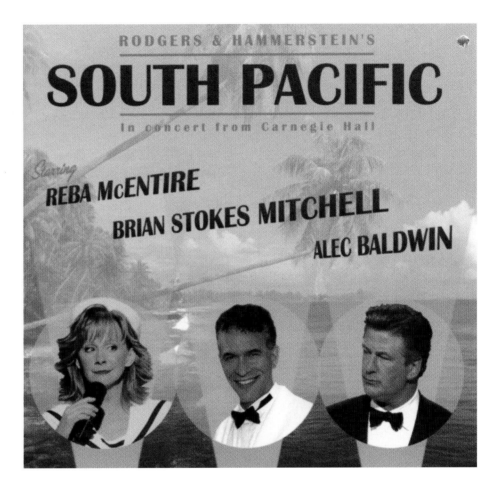

ingenuity is second to none as a director but here, perhaps, the ingenuity of the original creators trumped him; his alterations to the show's design did not seem to make it etter and the production was neither enthusiastically received nor restaged in America.

Coincidentally, Nunn's version was not the only reconstructed version to appear before the public in 2001. A brand-new television production, filmed on location in Australia, was broadcast on ABC on March 26. The elaborate telecast, which cost $15 million, starred stage and screen star Glenn Close as Nellie Forbush and featured Harry Connick, Jr., as Lieutenant Cable. Again, the structure of the show was altered to allow more sweeping visuals for the home screen, and for this version, the song "Happy Talk" was cut. Some of the changes infuriated purists, while other critics found it a fresh breeze to experience the

musical on screen without the color-saturated interludes of the film. Audiences seemed pleased; the broadcast placed in the Top Ten in that week's television ratings.

Still, even the high-profile of the television broadcast did not lead immediately to a New York revival—neither did a couple of well-produced national tours and productions in the 1980s and 1990s. Although these productions featured some first-class Broadway stars—among them, Robert Goulet, Richard Kiley, and Sandy Duncan, respectively— and there was some definite box-office appeal to them, they never gathered enough momentum to touch down on Broadway. *South Pacific* was such a special event of its time that it needed a special time to pave the way for its reappearance; as Ted Chapin, the president of the Rodgers and Hammerstein Organization, put it, "Of all the Rodgers and Hammerstein shows, it is the most connected to its

ABOVE, LEFT: Robert Goulet was a match in box office Heaven for the role of Emile de Becque. The romantic singing idol lent his vocal prowess to several revivals.

ABOVE, RIGHT: The acclaimed Carnegie Hall concert in 2005 brought together stars from the worlds of country/western music, Broadway, and the movies. Its public television broadcast went on to win an Emmy award

ABOVE, TOP: A particularly attractive poster for a revival at New Jersey's Paper Mill Playhouse.

ABOVE, BOTTOM: Kelli O'Hara and Paulo Szot are the new romantic team for the Lincoln Center Theater revival.

time. How do you get an audience back to that post-World War II era?" One trial balloon was floated on June 9, 2005; a special one-night-only concert version was staged at New York's fabled Carnegie Hall. Country-western singer Reba McEntire had scored such a success on Broadway several seasons earlier in a revival of *Annie Get Your Gun* that she kindled the enthusiasm of Rodgers' daughter, Mary, to see her as Nellie—besides, McEntire was raised in McAlester, Oklahoma, a few hours drive from Little Rock, Arkansas. McEntire was paired with the current golden voice of Broadway, Brian Stokes Mitchell as Emile and Alec Baldwin clowned around as Luther Billis. For those lucky few thousand crammed into Carnegie Hall, the score "was performed in a state of nearly unconditional rapture," according to the *New York Times*. (That Mr. Mitchell is himself an African American did not seem to noticeably derail the logic of the proceedings or the plot; apparently concerts have their own rules as well.)

In the wake of that concert, it seemed inevitable that *South Pacific* would return to Broadway—and in April 2008, as far up Broadway as you can possibly be and still be "on Broadway," it did—at the Lincoln Center Theater, a prestigious not-for-profit theater lodged between the Metropolitan Opera and Avery Fisher Hall. Through the vagaries of various production contracts, Lincoln Center Theater functions as an official Broadway venue, even though it is more than twenty blocks uptown from the center of New York's Theater District. Its main hall, the Vivian Beaumont, was designed in the 1960s by Jo Mielziner, the same designer who designed the original *South Pacific* in 1949, and has proven a hospitable venue for many musicals, including Hytner's revival of *Carousel*. Lincoln Center's artistic director, Andre Bishop, had been enamored of *South Pacific* since childhood—it remains his favorite musical—and was eager to produce it, if the right way could be found.

Bishop phoned Ted Chapin to congratulate him on the Carnegie Hall concert and reminded him of his continued interest in the show. Bishop mentioned that if the same team which had created their 2005 production of the musical *The Light in the Piazza* with such specificity, artistry, and integrity could be reassembled, surely they would be the best team to bring *South Pacific* to life again; there was also a felicity in the notion that, if they could do such an impressive job staging Adam Guettel's score, imagine what they could do with his grandfather's score. Chapin concurred and Lincoln

Center Theater set about bringing back Sher, who has had an impressive career staging new and epic plays in the regional and Off-Broadway world, along with his designers—Michael Yeargan for sets, Catherine Zuber for costumes, as well as Ted Sperling as musical director. (Lincoln Center Theater had already presented *South Pacific* as a benefit concert in 2000, featuring George Hearn, Karen Ziemba, and Bill Murray as Billis.) The opening date was set for April 3 in the Beaumont, with a cast of 44 and a 30-piece orchestra. Kelli O'Hara, who was featured in Piazza, is starring as Nellie opposite Brazilian bass-baritone, Paulo Szot. Bloody Mary will be played by Loretta Ables Sayre, a nightclub singer imported from Hawaii for this production; according to Bishop, she was "charming, tender, and terrifying."

The serious venue of Lincoln Center is a perfect fit for the serious intentions of the musical. "If you read about the original production," said Bishop, "it was highly Stanislavsky-like in its character relationships, in its pauses, with a great deal of subtext." What appealed to him as a producer was the show's depiction, in the finale, of a "harmonious mixed family—part of what America is now, is that we live in a world of mixed families—and *South Pacific* gives us a vision for those possibilities." From Sher's point of view, it is a deeply naturalistic piece of musical theater, with a vast amount of serious dramatic views to explore within a historical context; Sher's childhood was as admittedly devoid of Broadway cast albums as Bishop's was full of them—"I was into the Grateful Dead"—so he brings no preconceptions about the show's role in musical theater history, other than a respect for the authors and for the musical demands of the show.

There have been some profound changes in the world of *South Pacific*'s historical descendants—the islands of the New Hebrides became the independent Republic of Vanuatu in 1980 (their official flag includes the logo of a ceremonial boar's tooth, and Season Five of television's reality series *Survivor* took place there) and the Seabees were back in the news in fall 2005 when nearly 3,000 of them were deployed to New Orleans and Gulfport to rebuild communities and utilities destroyed by Hurricane Katrina. But, the question remains, is the world of 2008 still receptive to the options and optimism proposed by *South Pacific*? After all, if a Broadway musical could change the world's view of prejudice, racism would have vanished in April 1949. Almost sixty years after its premiere, nearly a decade into a new century, there is still much to be carefully taught by that most eloquent and rhapsodic of "teachers"—*South Pacific*.

ABOVE: At the golden anniversary reunion, members of the original cast of South Pacific on stage at New York's Symphony Space.

They will live a long time, these men of the South Pacific. They had an American quality. They, like their victories, will be remembered as long as our generation lives. After that, like the men of the Confederacy, they will become strangers. Longer and longer shadows will obscure them, until their Guadalcanal sounds distant on the ear like Shiloh and Valley Forge.

James A. Michener, *Tales of the South Pacific*

★ 186 ★

FURTHER READING

Block, Geoffrey, ed. *The Richard Rodgers Reader*, Oxford University Press, New York, 2002.

Day, A. Grove, *James A. Michener*. Twayne Publishers, Boston, 1977.

Fordin, Hugh, *Getting to Know Him: A Biography of Oscar Hammerstein II*, Random House, New York, 1977.

Hammerstein II, Oscar, *Lyrics*, Hal Leonard Books, Milwaukee, 1985.

Jones, John Bush, "World War II and The Rodgers and Hammerstein Years," *Our Musicals, Our Selves*, Brandeis University Press, 2003.

Keegan, John, *Collins Atlas of World War II*, HarperCollins, London, 2006.

Klein, Christina, *Cold War Orientalism: Asia in the Middlebrown Imagination, 1945-1961*, University of California Press, Berkley, 2003.

Lingeman, Richard, *Don't You Know There's a War On?* Thunder's Mouth Press, New York, 2003.

Logan, Joshua, *Josh: My Up and Down, In and Out Life*, Delacorte Press, New York, 1976.

Logan, Joshua, *Movie Stars, Real People and Me*, Delacorte Press, 1978.

Mander, Raymond and Joe Mitchenson, *Musical Comedy*, Taplinger Publishing Co., New York, 1969.

Marston, Daniel, ed. *The Pacific War Companion*, Osprey Publishing, London, 2005.

Martin, Mary, *My Heart Belongs*, Morrow, New York, 1976.

May, Stephen J. *Michener: A Writer's Journey*, University of Oklahoma Press, Norman, 2005.

Michener, James A. *James A. Michener Retells South Pacific* (illustrated by Michael Hague), Harcourt Brace Jovanovich, New York, 1992.

Michener, James A. *Tales of the South Pacific*, Macmillan, New York, 1947.

Michener, James A. *The World is My Home: A Memoir*, Random House, New York, 1992.

Mordden, Ethan, *Rodgers and Hammerstein*, Harry N. Abrams, New York, 1992.

Morison, Samuel Eliot, *The Two Ocean War: A Short History of the U.S. Navy in the Second World War*, Little, Brown, Boston: 1962.

Pinza, Ezio, *An Autobiography*, Arno Press, New York, 1977.

Rodgers, Richard, *Musical Stages, An Autobiography*, Random House, New York, 1975.

Schading, Barbara, *A Civilian's Guide to the U.S. Military*, Writer's Digest Books, Cincinnati, Ohio, 2007.

Secrest, Meryle, *Somewhere for Me: A Biography of Richard Rodgers*, Knopf, New York, 2001.

Ward, Geoffrey C. and Ken Burns, *The War: An Intimate History*, Knopf, New York, 2007.

Wilk, Max, *Overture and Finale*, Back Stage Books, New York, 1999.

Recommended Recordings:

1949 Original Broadway Cast (Martin, Pinza); Sony

1958 Movie Soundtrack (Gaynor, Tozzi); Sony/BMG

1967 Music Theater of Lincoln Center (Henderson, Tozzi); Sony/BMG

1986 London Studio Cast (Te Kanawa/Carreras); Sony

1996 London Studio Cast (O'Hara, Diaz); Jay Records

2001 TV Soundtrack (Close, Sherbedgia); Sony

2005 Concert Cast (McEntire, Mitchell); Decca Broadway

Recommended DVDs:

Motion Picture – Collector's Edition – Twentieth Century Fox Home Entertainment (2006)

ABC–TV Version – Walt Disney Video (2001)

In Concert from Carnegie Hall – Rhino/Image (2006)

To learn more about *South Pacific* and the musicals of Rodgers & Hammerstein, visit www.rnh.com

INDEX

CREDITS

Key: t top, b bottom, l left, r right, c center
We would like to thank all the film production and distribution companies and photographers whose photographs appear in this book. We apologize in advance for any unintentional omission or neglect and will be pleased to insert the appropriate acknowledgement for any companies or individuals in any subsequent edition of this work.

Cover images: Front main picture Rodgers & Hammerstein Organization/ Photograph used courtesy of Samuel Goldwyn Films; background Getty Images/Greg Vaughn; Back l Photofest; c Art by James McMullan, courtesy of Lincoln Center Theater/© 2007 by James McMullan. Used with permission of Pippin Properties, Inc; r Rodgers & Hammerstein Organization; Front inside flap Rodgers & Hammerstein Organization; Back inside flap Tess Steinkolk; Endpapers: Drop design for Bali Ha'i transformation in South Pacific 1948-1949. Watercolor on paper/Collection of the McNay Art Museum, Gift of Robert L. B. Tobin.

Alamy /Sylvia Cordaiy Picture Library/Nick Rains 28-29; AP/PA Photos 168, /U.S. Army Signal Corps 59t, /Matty Zimmerman 70; Corbis 59b, /Bettmann 20-21, 26, 32b, 40-41, 50, 55b, 64, 93, 153, /Horace Bristol 33b, 84, /CinemaPhoto 12br, /Jack Fields 83, /K. J. Historical/David Pollack 39, /Hulton-Deutsch Collection 14, 125, 169tl, /Fenno Jacobs 72, /The Mariners' Museum 38, /Anders Ryman 73, /John Springer Collection 100, /Werner Forman 82t; Getty Images /Hulton Archive/Kurt Hutton 104, 135, 145-146t, 155tr, 157, /National Geographic/Carsten Peter 2-3, /Terry O'Neill 147t, /Time & Life Pictures 32t, 33t, 36, 68, 98, 127t, 186; The Kobal Collection 164, 173; Library of Congress 66-67, 82b, /Oscar Hammerstein II Collection, Music Division 114, 126b, 127br, 162l, 169b, /Richard Rodgers Collection, Music Division, Library of Congress 45; Courtesy of Lincoln Center Theater /art by James McMullan 178, /set sketch by Michael Yeargan 146b, /costume sketch by Catherine Zuber 12t; Collection of the McNay Art Museum, Gift of Robert L. B. Tobin 78-79; Joan Marcus /© 2007 184b; Laurence Maslon 176; Museum of the City of New York/Theater Collection 34t, 113, 122, 141, 175; National Archives and Records Administration 31, 163; Photofest 6, 16, 18-19, 23, 61, 77, 89, 103, 106, 109-111, 127bl, 128-131, 137, 142, 152t, 159-161, 166-167, 170-171, 177, 180-181, 182b; Rodgers & Hammerstein Organization 1, 5, 11, 12bl, 17, 25, 34b, 43, 53-54, 57, 69, 71, 75, 80, 90-92, 97, 108, 116-119, 121, 124, 126t, 132-133, 136, 138-140, 147b, 148-151, 152b, 155tl, 158, 162r, 169tr, 172, 182t, 183l, 184t, 185, /used courtesy of Decca

Broadway 183r; Billy Rose Theater Division/The New York Public Library for the Performing Arts, Astor, Lenox and Tilden Foundations 55t; Anita & Steve Shevett 9-10; TopFoto.co.uk 155b, /ArenaPal /Peter Jones 62b, 120, /Public Record Office/HIP 48-49, /Topham Picturepoint 46, 62t, 156; Courtesy University of Northern Colorado Archives /Reprinted with the permission of Scribner, an imprint of Simon & Schuster Adult Publishing Group, from *Tales of the South Pacific* by James Michener. © 1946, 1947 by the Curtis Publishing Company. © 1947 by James A. Michener, renewed © 1975 by James A. Michener 94.

ACKNOWLEDGEMENTS

Let me first thank Ted Chapin and Bert Fink of the Rodgers and Hammerstein Organization, the Captain Brackett and Commander Harbison of this operation. Their support for this project, their careful and considered guidance, their patience and support set a high standard for collaboration. Bruce Pomahac, Carol Cornicelli and Kara Darling from R&H also gave unstintingly of their knowledge, experience and time—many thanks.

Kate Burkhalter of Anova Books was her usual charming, kind, and unflustered self—even through the maddeningly incorporeal world of e-mails and early morning phone conversations. I am extremely grateful for the inclusion of Emma O'Neill on this project—her diligence and discretion while coordinating the photographs and illustrations were a pleasure and the results apparent to any reader.

This book could never have been accomplished without the expert and enthusiastic research of Jennifer Tepper. Whether or not she was carefully taught I cannot say; she certainly got her knowledge and spirit *somewhere*. Karyn Gerhard was again there when I needed her; I thank her for her counsel. Tom Lindblade, Fritz Brun, Michael Kantor, and my father, Gerald Maslon, gave support and advice at crucial points in the journey. Jeff Posternak at the Wylie Agency was expert at bridging the gap across the pond.

Stephen J. May, the expert biographer of James Michener, helped on several crucial factual and visual fronts; I am particularly grateful for his navigation through the murky mists of Michener's own historical obfuscations.

I had the honor of speaking to Don Fellows, a *South Pacific* veteran, only days before he passed away. I was touched by his desire, even in his illness, to communicate the joy of that first production and I thank Robin Wood for arranging the conversation.

Mark Eden Horowitz, of the Library of Congress' Music Division, was once the again the epitome of a friend and a scholar—I also thank him for sharing his thoughts of the musical aspects of *South Pacific*. Alison Lotvin Birney and Jeffery Flannery of the LOC's Manuscript Division; Marty Jacobs of the Museum of the City of New York; and Jeremy Megraw of the Billy Rose Collection of the New York Public Library all helped to accommodate the insanely necessary speed of the book. Jere Couture opened the door to some important items in the Joshua Logan estate. Ron Mandelbaum of Photofest once again encouraged me to think the book was a worthwhile proposition. Thanks to Jonathan Tunick for sharing his thoughts; Sia Balabanovna for her life-saving map work; Philip Rinaldi of LCT for his time and attention; and Adam Guettel for lending his fine words to a perceptive foreword.

Andre Bishop and Bartlett Sher both gave of their much-coveted time to talk about their 2008 revival at Lincoln Center Theater, for which I am very grateful.

Finally, love and gratitude to my wife, Genevieve Elam. Ever since she, young and smiling, climbed up my hill, my life has been one of undiluted happiness. I can't wait for the future, which will be filled with the sound of her laughter, at the very least.

LM